The Options Trading

The Ultimate Guide For High Probabili

By Kiril Valtchev

TABLE OF CONTENTS

The Options Trading Bible®
The Ultimate Guide For High Probability Options Trading

By Kiril Valtchev

If you are interested in learning everything about futures, stocks, options, ETF'S and forex pick up a copy of the Trading Bible. This is another one of my books that is meant to help you learn all the different markets so you can get a better idea of how they interact with one another. You will not be disappointed.

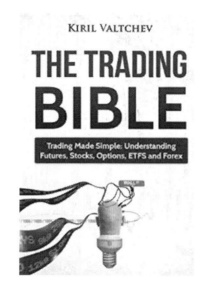

INTRO

Hello and thank you for picking up a copy of "The Options Trading Bible". Since you purchased this book you have an obvious interest in trading and making money. Options can be one of the most dynamic and efficient trading instrument around. They present the best investment and trading opportunities with limited capital.

Many people buy stocks and hold them for the long term in order to collect dividends and maybe see some appreciation in the value of their stock. This standard model can present massive risks to the average investor and leave them stranded with massive losses. To be honest this method is outdated, boring and riskier than most people have been taught.

Let me ask you this.

If you could collect rent on the stocks you already own would you do it? If you could minimize the risk in stocks you own would you do it? If you could learn to pick trades that have a 95% calculated probability of making you money would you do it?

I hope the answer to all these questions is YES. This book can help you do that and so much more.

This book is meant to help you understand options if you have never traded them before, if you actively trade them and or are an expert. By the time you finish reading this book you will have the knowledge and skills necessary to actively trade options, identify low risk and high probability trading scenarios, and even turn your loosing trades into winners.

The end goal with options is to help you make money in a much more controlled and predictable manner. You will not learn this overnight and if you want to make some serious money you will need to actively apply yourself.

Some of the best traders in the world are options traders and it is because they have become experts in identifying low risk and high probability trading scenarios. Become obsessed with learning all you can about options and you will start to see the money flood in.

Let's begin!!!

DISCLAIMER

The Options Trading Bible is for educational use only. Options trading has large potential rewards, but also large potential risks. You must be aware of the risks and be willing to accept them in order to invest and trade in the options market. Don't trade with money you can't afford to lose. This book is neither a solicitation nor an offer to Buy/Sell futures, spot forex, cfd's, options or other financial products.

No representation is being made that any account will or is likely to achieve profits or losses similar to those discussed in any material on this website. The past performance of any trading system or methodology is not necessarily indicative of future results. For the avoidance of any doubt, the Options Trading Bible and any associated companies, or employees, do not hold themselves out as Commodity Trading Advisors ("CTAs"). Given this representation, all information and material provided by the Options Trading Bible and any associated companies, or employees, is for educational purposes only and should not be considered specific investment advice.

CHAPTER 1: 10 TRADING RULES

Before we dive into options it is important to establish some mental and behavioral rules for trading. You must have mental and behavior rules in your trading or you will fail. These are much more important than most people realize. You can't allow yourself to become emotional with trading. You must hone your skills to become a logical and heartless creature when it comes to trading. Let's take a look at the 10 rules you should follow for your trading plan.

RULE (1) KNOW THE DIFFERENCE

You need to know the difference between a trade and an investment. You would be surprised as to how many people interpret a trade as an investment. A trade is a trade and it is meant to make you money in the short term. That's really it. If you deposit money at a brokerage firm and begin looking for possible short term moves in a stock you are looking for trades, not investments.

Investing focuses on building up wealth gradually over a longer period of time. The main focus is on compounding and reinvesting dividends and profits back into the same stock or portfolio. Investors focus on the overall fundamentals of company and its structure. Investors will stick through the downtrends in a stock or industry because they believe it will inevitably rebound and come back stronger.

Trading is short term. A trade can range from seconds, minutes, hours, days, weeks or even months. The frequency is what separates trading from investing. Traders rely on technical analysis and chart setups to identify good trading opportunities.

Investing and trading have the same end goal in mind, making money. They just do it in a slightly different way. It is important to distinguish between the two and always know which side you are on in order to be mentally prepared for the possible price fluctuations that may come from investing or trading.

RULE (2) LOSSES ARE LESSONS

Think of losses as lessons. They are okay if they happen straight out of the gate so it can humble your mentality and make you a risk-averse individual. If your first trade is a loss it can be a benefit to you because it will make you dig more to see what you did wrong. If your first trade is a winning trade, you are more likely to keep trading and not analyze what you just did. It is important to analyze both your loosing trades and your winning trades to make sure you are sticking to your trading rules.

Let's say for example that you bought 100 shares of Microsoft (MSFT) a month prior to their earnings being released because you believe that they have performed better this quarter than the previous. The stock begins to move against you and you become afraid that it could move even further away and cause bigger losses once earnings are actually released. You get out of the trade earlier and take a small loss.

Microsoft releases its earnings and they end up being much less than the previous quarter and the stocks drops 5%. Taking losses early on in a trade is good risk management because it limits your losses. If you had waited after earnings were released you would have lost even more. Don't be afraid to take losses early on, they are lessons that will help you become a better trader in the future.

RULE (3) REMOVE EMOTIONS

In order to become a consistently profitable trader you must learn to detach yourself from the emotional aspect of making and losing money. Money itself is never actually lost. It is simply transferred from one party to another. Begin to think of trading as a series of different transfers.

Trust me, I understand. Losing a trade is definitely a gut wrenching feeling. No one likes to lose money. It can shake you to your core. Making money on the other hand is exciting, exhilarating and empowering. It can boost your confidence and make you feel invisible.

The bad part about getting overly excited about making money in trading is that it can skew your logic and cause you to rely on your gut feeling for picking trades. This is when losses will begin to happen. I would suggest trading with an amount of money that you feel comfortable with, which if lost won't have a lifestyle impact on you.

Become excited about research, information and new ideas. As hard as it is, try your best to avoid getting emotional about making money or losing money. The sooner you begin to remove the emotion out of trading, the sooner you will see yourself becoming more and more profitable.

RULE (4) DON'T SHIFT

Adapt and follow your rules methodically. If you have identified a possible **"trade"**, make sure you keep it a trade. Sometimes people will get into a trade and once it starts becoming profitable they will decide to turn it into an investment. You must avoid doing this. Trades are meant to be trades and investments are meant to be investments. Once you begin shifting your methodology **mid-trade** you begin to lose sight of the original plan you had for that trade. Just because a trade is currently profitable doesn't mean it will continue on that path.

Once you enter into a trade make sure you treat it like a trade and not an investment. There is no worse feeling than seeing a profitable trade turn into a losing one because you decided to break your rules for just this one trade. The great thing about options which you will learn in a later chapter, is that you can turn your losing trades into profitable trades. Stick to your plans and adjust trade parameters, but do not turn them into investments.

RULE (5) DO YOUR OWN RESEARCH

At the end of the day it's your own money at stake. No one is going to care more about your money than you. You can find tips, tricks and plenty of other people's ideas on the internet for trades. Having been there myself I can tell you that majority of them suck. Why would anyone give out a profitable trade idea to the public? Most of the time if you see people online claiming that they have the next Apple or Amazon stock or the next obsolete trading strategy, they are trying to sell you something.

They are typically trying to sell you some sort of course or subscription. I would advise staying away. This is not the case with all of them. Some of them actually do provide valuable information. If you plan to subscribe to a trade service or newsletter do your homework. Compare different services and see what they offer first. Don't rely blindly on other people's trade ideas.

Do you think individual profitable traders actually have the time to create a website, create ads, courses and videos for trading? They typically keep to themselves and are buried in research at all times. It is important to get used to doing your own research so you can become a self-reliant and sufficient trader. You don't want to rely on other people for trade ideas and tips when you can generate them yourself. Take other people's ideas into consideration when making trading decisions, but at the end of the day rely on your own ideas and research. This is the best way to become a professional trader.

RULE (6) DON'T ALWAYS FOLLOW THE CROWD

You have to know that you can make money in any market condition. It does not matter how the overall market is performing, you can still find profitable ideas. During different market conditions some people may be more inclined to trade a certain industry because the overall market is shifting that way. Just because the market is moving a certain direction doesn't mean that you should default your thinking that you must do the same. Majority of traders lose money. There is a reason as to why they lose money and that is because they follow the crowd.

The crowd is not always wrong, but if you blindly follow market moves because the rest of the market says so, you will not be consistently profitable. You have to teach yourself to search and develop unique trading strategies that are not easily seen by the masses. This is how you become a consistently profitable trader.

RULE (7) LIMIT YOUR LOSSES

This one should be a no brainer. But time and time again, people overlook the simple concepts that are vital to trading. The quicker you cut your losses, the less money you end up losing. You can adjust your trade parameters once a trade is profitable and let the profits continue, that is easy. Let your winners be winners, but practice on containing your losses. It is hard for many traders to cut losses quickly. Their mentality operates under the notion that the trade will eventually turn around.

What if it doesn't? The worst thing is being stuck in a trade that you don't want to close because you will lose a ton of money. Learn to accept the fact that losses are a part of trading, but also hone your skills to cut losses quickly before they spiral out of control. Capital preservation and consistent growth is the lifeline for long term profitable trading.

RULE (8) CONTROL FEAR

The financial markets are an absolute massive infrastructure. They are full of thousands upon thousands of instruments, companies and combinations of trading. Rookie traders are often in fear of missing a trade and out of desperation they end up getting into trades too late or too early. Don't become scared that you missed out on a particular trade. There are thousands of others ones waiting to be discovered. Traders sometimes fear that just because they missed out on a really good trade it will be a long time before another one like it comes around. This is false. With options there are literally an endless amount of trade possibilities.

If you do your due diligence and search for trades every day, you will find more and more trade setups. Once you learn to control your fear of missing out on a trade you can continue looking and looking until the correct trade comes up. You never want to trade out of desperation. Some traders think that because they haven't executed a trade in a few days or weeks that they are missing out. This is not true. You have to understand that each trade costs you money, so the more and more you trade the more trading costs you will incur. You don't have to always be in a trade. It is good to sit back and evaluate how a certain security is performing and see how the market moves. Use your fear to your advantage and control it.

RULE (9) DON'T TRADE THE HEADLINES

You will rarely make money long term if you only trade the headlines. You might get lucky from time to time and hit a few winning trades, but if you only trade the headlines you will see your account shrink long term. Headlines won't give you strategies, they give you a consensus. The people who write the headlines are typically columnist or contributors, they aren't actually traders themselves. Why would you ever take advice from someone who is not a trader themselves? You can use the headlines as a basis to gain a general outlook on a particular equity, but don't use it as the sole determining factor to make your trading decision.

This goes back to rule number 6. It's pretty much following the crowd, which you should avoid. Headlines are meant to be cautions and updates, not a basis for reaction. Don't read into the headlines too much because they are typically biased written opinions that can shift your focus. Once we dig into options you will see how to avoid the headlines and focus on logic and statistics. Logic and statistics are a recipe for making consistent profits in trading. Headlines can cause emotions in trading because the people who write them are trying to invoke emotions out of people. That's what writers do. They try to invoke an emotional response from people. Follow the formula below and you will learn to rely on yourself and not the headlines.

(Logic + Statistics – Emotion) = Profitable Trading

RULE (10) AVOID TRADING FLOW ONLY

There is nothing wrong with reading the tape of a stock or level 2 quotes. It can actually give you a deeper insight into the daily price behavior of a stock. Many rookie traders rely too much on level two pricing and tape reading for making trade decisions. They use it as their main indicator to get into a specific trade. If you are planning on completely day trading and not holding any overnight positions, level 2 quotes and tape reading are your best guides.

You must be extremely careful if you plan to never hold any overnight positions. You must be very cost conscious and be 100% certain that your broker has laser fast execution or else you can get punished with fees. Trading flow can be profitable in the short term, but long term you shouldn't rely solely on volume and price. There are many other factors to consider before entering into an intelligent trade.

Make sure to use these 10 rules as mental preparation for trading. The standards in these rules will remain the same, but you will have to periodically adjust them based on how the market moves and individual equities react. Now, let's dive into these options and learn what it will take to start making consistent profits.

CHAPTER 2: THE BASICS

Before we dive into the complexities of options it is important to understand what the options market actually is and how it works. Many people have heard about the options market but are very unfamiliar as to what it is and how it actually works. Let's take a look into the history of the options market and how it functions.

HISTORY OF OPTIONS

Many people think that options are a new trading product, but they are terribly wrong. The very first options contracts date back to ancient Greece and were used to speculate on the olive harvest. The story begins with Thales and the Olive harvest.

Thales of Miletus was a philosopher in ancient Greece who had profited from an olive harvest. He had a strong interest in mathematics, astronomy and economics. With his knowledge and strong interest of math, astronomy and economics he essentially created the very first options contract. By studying the stars, Thales predicted that there would be big olive harvest in his area and went on to profit from his speculation. He predicted that there would be a strong demand for olive presses and basically wanted to own the market for them.

The only problem was that he didn't have enough money to buy all the olive presses. What he ended up doing is paying all the owners of the presses a sum of money in order to have the rights to use them at harvest season. When harvest season came around the corner, Thales's prediction of a large harvest was right. The harvest ended up being massive. Needless to say the demand for olive presses went up. He ended up reselling his rights to the olive presses to people who wanted them and made a healthy profit. This type of deal was not common and by doing so Thales essentially created the first call option with the olive presses acting as the underlying asset.

Another instance of options trading in history is Tulip Mania in 17th century Holland. This is commonly known and referred to as **"Tulip Bulb Mania".** During the 17th century, tulips were very popular in the Holland region and were a status symbol in the Dutch community. Their popularity slowly spread throughout Europe and the rest of the world, which inevitably led to a massive increase in their demand.

During this time in history, call options and put options were being used in different markets, mainly to hedge price fluctuations. For example, tulip growers bought **"puts"** as protection for their profits in case the price of tulip bulbs went down. The tulip wholesalers bought **"calls"** as protection against the price of tulip bulbs going up. The options contracts that were created back then were not standardized and were completely unregulated.

The price of tulip bulbs continued to rise over the years and eventually the bubble popped. Tulip prices had gotten so high that they became unsustainable. The buyers began to slowly dwindle away as the prices began to tank. People who had risked everything they had on tulips were completely wiped out. People lost their savings, houses and livelihoods.

At this point the Dutch economy slid into a recession. Since the options market at that time was unregulated and non-transparent, there wasn't a due process to make investors fulfill their obligations on their options contracts. This gave options a bad reputation for the following years and transactions slowly decreased.

Shortly following the Tulip Bulb Mania crash, options began to get banned in several parts of the world including: Europe, Japan and some major states in the US. They were still very appealing to many investors because they offered great leverage. Traders still continued to trade them where they could but their bad reputation kept their transaction volume low. They eventually got permanently banned and made illegal in the 18th century. This lasted over 100 years until they were resurrected back in the 19th century by a man named Russell Sage.

Russell Sage was a notable American financier in the late 19th century who created a way to trade options over the counter in the United States. What Sage did was essentially create the relationship of pricing between options and their underlying assets. What Sage did was use the principle of a put call parity to devise synthetic loans that were then created to buy shares of stock and a related put option from a customer. This allowed Sage to loan money to people and set the interest rate that he wanted by fixing the price of the contracts and their strike prices. This led to significant losses and Sage eventually stopped trading this way. Sage was a key figure in the development of options pricing and trading.

During the 1800's, brokers and dealers began to place advertisements in newspapers to pull in buyers and sellers of options contracts with a view of the available deals that were getting priced. They hoped that the interested party would call the broker and buy either calls or puts on a particular equity. The broker would then try to find another person willing to take the opposite side of that transaction. The process was slow and cumbersome. This eventually led to the formation of the Dealers Association. The terms of the contracts were determined by the two parties. The contracts were not standardized or regulated during that time. Since they were unregulated many investors remained wary which led to thin volume.

The options market continued to be controlled and run by the **Dealers Association,** with the options contracts being traded over the counter. The contracts slowly started to become more standardized and people became more educated on their functionality and investment potential. The activity slowly began to pick as more options were introduced on different equities. The brokers in the Dealers Association made their money from the spread between the buyers and the sellers of the options contracts. Since there was a lack of regulation and standardization in the contracts, the pricing on the options contracts didn't have a good structure. The brokers could price out the contracts with very wide spreads. Investors still didn't see options as a viable investing instrument.

In late 1960's, the **Chicago Board of Trade** began to see a major drop in trading volume for commodity futures and it began to look for new ways to continue its growth. Their goal was to offer more instruments for trading so they could diversify the base of their offerings to the public. After much thought and consideration they decided to create an exchange for trading options. This would not be an easy task.

In 1973, **the Chicago Board of Options Exchange (CBOE)** was open for trading. Options contracts were officially standardized and had proper pricing structure. To make things even better, the Options Clearing Corporation was also formed to regulate and oversee the clearing and fulfillment of options contracts. This helped to legitimize the trading of options and investors were now fully confident in using them as a solid investment.

Over the next following decades the options market continue to change and evolve with options being offered on different instruments and markets. More options exchanges were introduced and trading volume picked up exponentially. By the end of the 20th century, online trading began to gain massive interest and popularity.

Trading that was once available to a select few was now available to the general public. Online brokers began to pop up left and right and professional and newbie traders could now sit behind their laptops and fire off trades. The options market exploded and volumes grew to historical levels. At the end of 2015, the CBOE boasted an annual trading volume of 1.27 billion contracts traded. The CBOE now offers options on over 2,300 companies, 22 stock indices and over 140 ETF's. The evolution of options from where it began to where it is today is a remarkable feat. So now that you have a bit of history of how options began and where they are today, let's take a look at what they actually are and how they work.

WHAT IS AN OPTION?

An option is a contract in which a seller gives a buyer the right, but not the obligation, to buy or sell a specific number of shares at a predetermined price within a set period of time. Options are derivatives. This means their value is derived from the value of an underlying asset or investment. The most common underlying investment on which options are based is shares in a publicly traded company. Options contracts also exist in stock indexes, ETF's, government securities, currencies and even futures. So how much does 1 options contract represent? One options contract is equivalent to 100 shares of stock.

1 options contract = 100 shares of stock

Let's take a look into a real life example of how an options contract works.

__House Example__

You are out house hunting and you have finally landed on the property that you would love to purchase. The only issue is that you won't have the cash you need to buy it for the next 6 months. You talk to the seller and strike a deal that gives you an option to purchase the house in 6 months for a price of $500,000. The seller agrees, but for this option you pay a price of $10,000. Consider the following factors that might arise.

1.) You find out that the house was the original birthplace of Marlon Brando (a famous actor). As a result, the market value of the house explodes to $2 million. Since the seller sold you the option, he is under obligation to sell you the house for the $500,000 that you agreed upon. You stand to make a healthy profit of **$1,490,000**. Not too shabby!

($2,000,000 - $500,000 - $10,000)= **$1,490,000**

2.) While living in the house you discover that the attic has a significant amount of mold and that the roof is beginning to cave in. You now consider the house to be worthless. The good thing is that you didn't buy the house, you bought an option. You are not under any obligation to purchase the house. The only bad part is that you lose your $10,000 that you put down for the option.

This example illustrates two important parts of options contracts.

1.) You have a right to purchase the option, but not an obligation. The great thing about options is you can always let the expiration date go by, at which point the option becomes worthless. You will however lose 100% of the money you used to purchase the option.
2.) Options are derivatives. They derive their value from an asset. In our case the value of the option was derived by the house.

WHY TRADE OPTIONS?

Options aren't the right investment vehicle for everyone. Options can be very risky and complicated, but at the same time provide considerable opportunities to profit for individuals who know how to use them to their full potential. Options trading can provide many different advantages over other trading instruments. Below are some of their advantages over other instruments.

- Limited Risk
- Leverage
- Insurance
- Flexibility

LIMITED RISK

A huge advantage of trading options over direct equities is having the ability to significantly limit your downside risk while having unlimited profit potential. This goes back to the idea of options buyers having the right, but not the obligation, to execute a contract for an underlying asset. If the price of the asset is not what the buyer originally projected at the time of expiration, the buyer simply forfeits their right and just lets the contact expire worthless. They will lose their original investment for which they paid the right to own the option, but they only lose the amount they put in and know their max loss right from the start.

LEVERAGE

When a buyer of an options contract enters a deal they pay an amount to the options seller known as the premium (we will go into deep details about the options premium in another section).The premium is just the sum that is paid to the seller for the option. When an option is bought, you aren't buying anything or owning anything. An asset is not transferred unless the buyer chooses to exercise the option. The value of the contract, as we have said before, is determined by the underlying asset or security. For this example we will use Apple shares.

Options contracts have different contract multipliers depending on which class of options they fall in. These are determined by the exchanges themselves. For our example we will use the standard of 1 options contract being equivalent to 100 shares of stock. Each options contract would give you the right to purchase 100 shares of stock from the options seller.

So, if you purchased 5 options contracts on Apple, it means you can purchase 500 shares of Apple at expiration if you decide that the price is what you want. **(5 x 100).** Options give you great leverage. You can use options to have control of 100 shares of stock without having to put up the full capital of actually owning 100 shares of stock. When you buy a stock straight up you by the stock price times the number of shares you purchased. If you purchased a long call option, you would pay the long call premium multiplied by the 100 shares that the option controls.

Example

Long $100 call in Apple for $2.50

*We would pay $2.50 x 100 shares = **$250***

Other countries have different contract multipliers. It is important to look at the contract specs of an option prior to trading. Option trading is very alluring to smaller investors because it gives them the opportunity to control a large amount of stock while only putting up a small amount of capital.

INSURANCE

Another way traders or investors may use options is as an insurance policy for their portfolio. They can give investors methods to protect their downside risk in case of drastic price declines and or crashes. An example of this would be a protective put, which we will get into in another section.

FLEXIBILITY

The great thing about options is that they have the ability to help you create a dynamic and custom portfolio structure. You can carry out many different trading strategies that will help you profit no matter if the price of an asset is going up, down, or consolidating. When you trade stocks you are limited to price fluctuations.

With the many different options strategies like strangles, straddles, covered calls and iron condors, you can profit from the stock even if it stays flat. With options you can calculate your risk, evaluate your market assumptions, and create a robust trading strategy that fits you risk appetite.

WHO TRADES OPTIONS?

Who are they? Who are some of the players in the options markets? People who trade options are in the market for two reasons: to avoid risk and to take on risk. Some of the players in the market include the following below.

- Retail traders
- Prop Firms
- HFT Shops
- Market Makers
- Hedge Funds
- Portfolio managers

RETAIL TRADERS

Retail traders are generally people who have a small to mid -size account at an online retail broker of some sort like TD-Ameritrade, Scott Trade, or Fidelity to name a few. Most retail traders trade their own money at their own discretion. They primarily trade options to speculate and are thought of as non-professionals in the trading industry.

PROP FIRMS

Prop firms or prop traders are traders who trade for banks and large institutions. They deploy a wide range of different strategies in order to make money. Prop firms trade portfolios anywhere from 100 million dollars and above.

HFT SHOPS

HFT stands for High Frequency Trading. This is a style of trading involves using complex trading strategies that are typically fully automated through the use of an algorithm. HFT shops are companies which use algorithms to trade. They focus on arbitrage opportunities that may present themselves in the market. They require significant amount of capital, infrastructure, and highly competent programmers in order to operate. Their fund size can range anywhere from 500 million to as much as 5 billion. A very popular HFT shop is Renaissance Technologies.

MARKET MAKERS

Market makers are essential to the market, specifically options markets. They are the primarily volume contributor when it comes to options. They are trading firms or institutions which have an obligation to the exchanges to provide pricing on options contracts in return for a reduced exchange fee. They provide the bid/ask prices on options contracts which gives assurance to traders that their trades will get a reasonable fill. Not all firms are incentivized by the exchanges.

HEDGE FUNDS

Hedge funds are alternative investments using accredited investors funds to trade many different strategies in order to produce a return. Their interests are completely aligned with their investors because they make more money when they have a positive return. Most hedge funds operate under the 2/20 fee structure. They have a 2% management fee for all the funds they manage and a 20% performance fee. The performance fee is assessed if the fund returns 20% for the year. Hedge funds are highly incentivized to perform well because they will end up making more money.

PORTFOLIO MANAGERS

A portfolio manager is a trader, or a group of traders who trade on behalf of someone else. They can be investment managers of global banks, managers of ETF's, mutual fund managers, and pension fund managers. Portfolio managers will typically hold equities along with some long term options contracts. They trade massive volumes in a single trade.

RISK OF TRADING OPTIONS

Trading is not without risk. Option trading has great benefits along with great risks. Options can be very risky but they can also provide unique trading opportunities to profit for people who learn to properly use them. Options have certain characteristics that make them less attractive for certain type of traders and investors. Let's take a look at some of them below:

- Time Sensitive Investments
- Non-Tangible
- Complex

TIME SENSITIVE INVESTMENTS

Options are very time sensitive investments. A typical options contract is usually held for short period of time- typically a few weeks to a few months. There are longer term options available from one to two years, but they are not as popular to most retail traders. A buyer of an options contract could lose their entire investment even if they correctly predict where the value of an asset will go, if it doesn't happen within the set time frame of the options contract.

NON-TANGIBLE

Options contracts are less tangible than stocks and other investments. Stocks offer investors certificates as proof of ownership, but options are essentially a ticket stamp on a trade and don't provide any form of ownership.

COMPLEX

Options can get extremely complicated because they are so versatile. Buying shares in a stock is very straightforward. You simply log into your brokerage account, select the stock you want to buy, the number of shares and you click execute. Before you get into an options trade there are a multitude of variables that you must consider before actually getting into a trade. First and foremost you must decide if you are going to execute a **call** or a **put**. Some of the other parts to an options contract to consider are as follows:

- Strike Price

- Options Premium
- Money-ness of an Option
- Expiration
- Exercise & Assignment
- Implied Volatility
- Earnings

With all these parts to consider before getting into an options trade, it is important to fully understand them and how they interact with one another. By knowing how all the parts of an option contract relate to the price of the asset, you will be equipped with the skills necessary to make a good trading decision.

CHAPTER 3: OPTIONS DECODED

Now that we have working knowledge of what an option is and how it works, we can now dive deep into the different types of options and their structure. It is extremely important that you become an expert about everything in this chapter. This chapter will be your baseline for understanding options. There are only two types of options contracts, calls and puts.

CALL OPTION

A call option is an options contract in which the buyer has the right, but not the obligation, to **buy** a certain quantity of a security at a specified price within a fixed period of time. Buyers of call options are called **holders.**

A seller of a call option is known as a **writer.** If you are the writer of call option you have an obligation to sell the underlying security at the **strike price** if the option gets exercised. The writer of the call option will get paid a **premium** for taking risk on the option. The premium is the cost basis for the holder of the option.

BUYING A CALL

Buying a call option is the easiest method to trade call options. New traders usually start off their options trading by buying calls. Call options are simple and they can generate decent returns if the underlying security moves in your favor. Let's take a look at the following example for a better understanding.

Example

*Let's say that the stock price of Microsoft (**MSFT**)is currently trading at $40/share. A call option contract with a strike price of $40 expiring in a month is being priced at $2. You have reason to believe that **MSFT** will go up in price in the next few weeks. So you pay $200 to purchase one $40 MSFT call option.*

1 options contract = 100 shares   *100 x $2= $200*

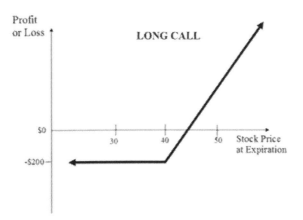

*Let's say your prediction was spot on and **MSFT** rallies to $50/share. In this example your trade would net you $800.*

*If you decided to exercise your call option, you declare your right to buy 100 shares of **MSFT** at $40/share and sell them for $50/share. This would net you $10/share. Since 1 options contract controls 100 shares of stock, you will receive $1,000 when you exercise the option.*

You paid $200 to buy the call option, so you net $800. If you only purchased shares in the stock, you would net 25% on this trade. A call option ends up getting you 400%ROI in this scenario. You can't generate these types of returns if you bought shares in the stock directly. You would also have to put up a significant amount of margin to make this kind of cash from a$10 rise in the stock price.

SELLING A CALL

The great thing with options is that you are not limited to one direction. You can also sell call options. Call option sellers, also known as writers, sell call options with the intention that they will end up expiring worthless, so they can collect the premiums on them. This method can be risky, but very profitable if executed correctly. We will dive deeper into selling calls options in a later chapter.

CALL SPREADS

Remember we mentioned that options are versatile and flexible? A call spread is further proof that they are. A call spread is an options strategy in which a trader simultaneously buys and sells an equal amount of call options on the same underlying asset with different strike prices and the same expiration dates.

They are meant to limit losses and also limit the potential profit on a trade. Call spreads can be used in unique ways to turn trades around if they are going against you. We will be discussing the many different types of options spreads in a different chapter.

PUT OPTION

A put option is an options contract in which the buyer has the right, but not the obligation, to **sell** a certain quantity of a security at a specified price within a fixed period of time. Sellers of put options are called **writers**. If you are the writer of put option you have an obligation to buy the underlying security at the **strike price** if the option gets exercised. The writer of the put option is paid a **premium** for taking the risk on the option.

BUYING A PUT

Buying a put option is one of the easiest ways to trade put options. Some traders prefer to buy put options instead of buying call options. Like call options, put options can also generate decent returns if they underlying security moves in your favor. When you buy a put option, you are betting on the price of the stock going down. Let's take a look at the following example for a better understanding.

Example

*Let's say that the stock price of Microsoft (**MSFT**)is currently trading at $40/share. A put option contract with a strike price of $40 expiring in a* *month is being priced at $2. You have reason to believe that **MSFT** will go down in the next few weeks. So you paid $200 to purchase one $40 MSFT put option.*

1 options contract = 100 shares   *100 x $2= $200*

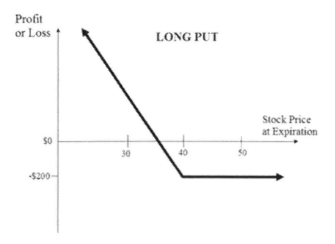

*Let's say your prediction was spot on and **MSFT** falls to $30/share. In this example your trade would net you $800.*

*If you decided to exercise your put option, you declare your right to sell 100 shares of **MSFT** at $40/share. This would net you $10/share. Since 1 options contract controls 100 shares of stock, you will receive $1,000 when you exercise the option.*

You paid $200 to buy the put option, so you net $800. If you only purchased shares in the stock, you would net 25% on this trade. A put option ends up getting you 400%ROI in this scenario. You can't generate these types of returns if you bought shares in the stock directly. You would also have to put up a significant amount of margin to make this kind of cash from a$10 drop in the stock price.

SELLING A PUT

Instead of buying a put option, you can sell a put option. Put option sellers, also known as writers, sell put options with the intention that they will end up expiring worthless, so they can collect the premiums on them. When you sell put options, you are betting that the price of the stock will go up in price. Selling put options can also be risky, but very profitable if executed correctly. We will take a look at the different combinations of put options in a later chapter.

PUT SPREADS

A put spread is an options strategy in which a trader simultaneously buys and sells an equal amount of put options on the same underlying asset with different strike prices on the same expiration date.

Like call spreads, put spreads are meant to limit losses and also limit the potential profit on a trade. Put spreads are a unique way to hedge your long term risk in a particular equity. We will be going over different put spread trade setups in a later chapter.

OPTION STYLE

In options trading, the style of an option falls into two different categories. Options will fall either into European or American style options. The difference between the two options comes to when the options can be exercised.

A European option can be exercised only at the expiration date of the option at a pre-determined point in time. An American style option can be exercised at any time before the expiration date. Almost all equity options are American style options. Generally index options are European style.

STRIKE PRICE

The strike price is the price at which the buyer (**holder**) of an option can buy or sell the underlying security when the option is exercised. The strike price can also be referred to as the exercise price.

For call options, the strike price is where the underlying security can be bought. For put options, the strike price is where the underlying security can be sold. The strike price affects the **money-ness** of an option and it's the primary determinant of the option's premium.

It is important to understand the relationship between the strike price and the call option price. For call options, the higher the strike price, the cheaper the option will be. The call options price table shows the option premiums that are typical for call options at different strike prices when the underlying security is trading at $80.

Call Option Price Table

Strike Price	Money-ness	Call Option Premium	Intrinsic Value	Time Value
60	ITM	17	10	7
70	ITM	14.5	8	6.5
75	ITM	12	4	8
80	ATM	9.5	0	9.5
85	OTM	7	0	7
90	OTM	4.5	0	4.5
95	OTM	2	0	2

You can see that as the strike price increases, the cheaper the call options premium becomes. As the strike price decreases on call options, the call options premium increases. The strike price along with the current market price determines if the option has any intrinsic value.

It is also important to understand the relationship between the strike price and the put option price. For put options, the higher the strike price, the more expensive the option will be. The put options price table shows the option premiums that are typical for put options at different strike prices when the underlying security is trading at $80.

Put Option Price Table

Strike Price	Money-ness	Put Option Premium	Intrinsic Value	Time Value
60	OTM	2	0	2
70	OTM	4.5	0	4.5
75	OTM	7	0	7
80	ATM	9.5	0	9.5
85	ITM	12	4	8
90	ITM	14.5	8	6.5
95	ITM	17	10	7

You can see that as the strike price increases, the more expensive the put options premium becomes. As the strike price decreases, the put options premium decreases.

OPTION PREMIUM

The option premium is simply the price paid to the seller to get the option. If you are the seller (**writer**) of the options contract you will receive the premium if the options contract expires worthless. As the seller of an options contract, you want the contract to expire worthless. The options premium is determined by the **intrinsic value**, **time value** and the **options volatility**.

INTRINSIC VALUE

The intrinsic value is the difference between the current trading price of the asset and the strike price.

Intrinsic Value = Current Trading Price – Strike Price

The only options that have intrinsic value are in-the-money (**ITM**) options. Out-of-the-money (**OTM**) options have no intrinsic value.

TIME VALUE

The time value of an option depends up on the amount of time that is remaining to exercise the option, the **money-ness** of the option, and the volatility of the underlying asset's market price. As the expiration date of an option approaches, the time value of an option decreases. This is known as time decay. As so, options are coined as wasting assets. The rate at which an option decays is known as the **theta.**

Theta is meant to show how quickly an option loses its value as the expiration date approaches. It is typically shown as a negative number. The theta shows the amount by which the option's value will decrease every day.

Example

A call option is currently priced at $5 and has a theta of **(-.10)**. This means that the price of the option will drop **$.10** every day. So after 3 days pass, the price of the option will fall to $4.70.

The theta is higher for shorter term options and lower for longer term options.

OPTIONS VOLATILITY

Options volatility consists of two parts, **implied volatility** and **historical volatility.**

Implied volatility is an integral part to options trading. It is the driving force behind options pricing and it's crucial to understand if you want to have profitable trades. Implied volatility is a market sentiment of where volatility in a particular equity should be in the near future. It shows how volatile the market may be in the near future and it can help you calculate the probability for a winning trade.

This is critical in helping you determine the probability that a certain stock will reach a certain price within a set period of time. While implied volatility gives you great insight into the markets opinion, you have to understand that it's not absolute, it's theoretical. By understanding implied volatility you can enter a trade knowing how the overall market feels about it. It does not forecast the future direction of an instrument. If implied volatility for a stock is high, the market believes that there is potential for large price movements in any direction. If the implied volatility for a stock is low, the market believes that the stock will not move much as the options nears expiration.

Historical volatility is the annualized standard deviation of past stock price movements. The historical volatility measures the daily price changes in a stock over the past year. It is used as a way to tell how far the stock has stretched in the past year. Historical volatility is good to know because it's something you can use to measure against implied volatility.

MONEY-NESS OF AN OPTION

The money-ness of an option is a term that is used to illustrate the relationship between the current trading price of the underlying security and its strike price. Let's take a look at some of the terms that describe this relationship.

ITM

ITM stands for **In-the-Money**. You don't have to overthink this for now. It will begin to click in other chapters when you see how options are priced. A **call option** is considered in-the-money when the strike price is below the current trading price of the underlying security. A **put option** is considered in-the-money when the strike price is above the current trading price of the underlying security.

Call Option = ITM (Strike Price < Current Trading Price)

Put Option = ITM (Strike Price > Current Trading Price)

You will notice that ITM options will tend be more expensive because their premium has significant intrinsic value along with their time value.

OTM

OTM stands for **Out-of-the-Money**. A **call option** is considered out-of-the-money when the strike price is above the current trading price of the underlying security. A **put option** is considered out-of-the-money when the strike price is below the current trading price of the underlying security.

Call Option = OTM (Strike Price > Current Trading Price)

Put Option = OTM (Strike Price < Current Trading Price)

You can see from our earlier example from our option price tables that out-of-the-money options have zero intrinsic value. These options will be cheaper because their probability of expiring worthless is high.

ATM

ATM stands for **At-the-Money**. A call or put option that has a strike price that is equal to the current trading price of the underlying security is considered at-the-money.

Call Option = ATM (Strike Price = Current Trading Price)

Put Option = ATM (Strike Price = Current Trading Price)

ATM options don't have any intrinsic value. They only have time value which is greatly impacted by the volatility in the underlying stock.

EXPIRATION

Options contracts have a limited life. Each options contract will be defined by an expiration date. The expiration date is the date on which the options contract becomes void and the right to exercise the options is no longer available. US stocks expire on the third Friday of the expiration month of the contract.

The only time that they don't expire on Friday is if it happens to be a holiday, in which case it will moved by one day to Thursday. It is important to know when your options contract will expire so you know your trade duration.

Options also have different expiration cycles. Different expiration dates apply to different series of options. The options cycle is the sequence of months in which the options contracts expire.

The different cycles apply to stock options, index options, futures options, commodity options and currency options. Below are the three different cycles.

*1st- January, April, July and October **(JAJO)***
*2nd – February, May, August and November **(FMAN)***
*3rd- March, June, September and December **(MJSD)***

There will always be at least four different expiration months available for stocks which have options available for trading.

This is what a typical expiration calendar looks like. The one below is for 2016.

JANUARY

S	M	T	W	T	F	S
					1	2
3	4	5	6	7	8	9
10	11	12	13	14	15	16
17	18	19	20	21	22	23
24	25	26	27	28	29	30
31						

FEBRUARY

S	M	T	W	T	F	S
	1	2	3	4	5	6
7	8	9	10	11	12	13
14	15	16	17	18	19	20
21	22	23	24	25	26	27
28	29					

MARCH

S	M	T	W	T	F	S
	1	2	3	4	5
6	7	8	9	10	11	12
13	14	15	16	17	18	19
20	21	22	23	24	25	26
27	28	29	30	31		

APRIL

S	M	T	W	T	F	S
					1	2
3	4	5	6	7	8	9
10	11	12	13	14	15	16
17	18	19	20	21	22	23
24	25	26	27	28	29	30

MAY

S	M	T	W	T	F	S
1	2	3	4	5	6	7
8	9	10	11	12	13	14
15	16	17	18	19	20	21
22	23	24	25	26	27	28
29	30	31				

JUNE

S	M	T	W	T	F	S
			1	2	3	4
5	6	7	8	9	10	11
12	13	14	15	16	17	18
19	20	21	22	23	24	25
26	27	28	29	30		

JULY

S	M	T	W	T	F	S
					1	2
3	4	5	6	7	8	9
10	11	12	13	14	15	16
17	18	19	20	21	22	23
24	25	26	27	28	29	30
31						

AUGUST

S	M	T	W	T	F	S
	1	2	3	4	5	6
7	8	9	10	11	12	13
14	15	16	17	18	19	20
21	22	23	24	25	26	27
28	29	30	31			

SEPTEMBER

S	M	T	W	T	F	S
				1	2	3
4	5	6	7	8	9	10
11	12	13	14	15	16	17
18	19	20	21	22	23	24
25	26	27	28	29	30	

OCTOBER

S	M	T	W	T	F	S
						1
2	3	4	5	6	7	8
9	10	11	12	13	14	15
16	17	18	19	20	21	22
23	24	25	26	27	28	29
30	31					

NOVEMBER

S	M	T	W	T	F	S
	1	2	3	4	5
6	7	8	9	10	11	12
13	14	15	16	17	18	19
20	21	22	23	24	25	26
27	28	29	30			

DECEMBER

S	M	T	W	T	F	S
				1	2	3
4	5	6	7	8	9	10
11	12	13	14	15	16	17
18	19	20	21	22	23	24
25	26	27	28	29	30	31

If you want further information about options expiration calendars, the website below has tons of information.

http://www.optionsclearing.com/about/publications/expiration-calendar-next-year.jsp

EXERCISE & ASSIGNMENT

What does it mean to exercise your option? To exercise an option means that you are executing your right to buy or sell the underlying security at the strike price. For the holder **(buyer)** of a call option it means they may exercise their right to buy the underlying security at the specified price. The specified price is the strike price. For the buyer of a put option it means that they may exercise their right to sell the underlying security at the specified price. There are a decent amount of options contracts that do not go all the way to expiration.

They are exercised prior to expiration for many different reasons. Sometimes an option may move significantly more than expected and traders end up exercising prior to expiration to lock in profits or cut losses. Sometimes they end up finding a better options trade and want to free up some margin so they can get in.

The list can get pretty lengthy. Another reason trades exercise options prior to expiration is because they are adjusting their strategy and incorporating different spreads into the trade plan to maximize the potential of the trade. We will get into options spreads in a later chapter.

Assignment in options occurs when the option is exercised by the options holder. The options seller **(writer)** is **"assigned"** to deliver the obligations under the options contract. Once a call option gets assigned, the options seller will have to sell the specified quantity of the underlying security at the strike price.

Once a put option gets assigned, the options seller will have to buy the specified quantity of the underlying security at the strike price. You don't have to think too much about assignment in options because they will be auto-filled when you trade them online. There will be nothing manual done on your end for assignment.

Next we will dive into the different types of orders and margin requirements for options contracts.

CHAPTER 4: READING AN OPTIONS CHAIN

It is important to note that not all stocks have options listed for trading. Many people assume that every stock has tradable options contracts. In order for a stock to be eligible for options trading there must be some requirements that need to be met. Publicly traded companies must meet the four following criteria below in order to be eligible to trade options:

- The stock must be listed on NYSE, NASDAQ or AMEX
- The closing price of the stock must have a minimum per share price for majority of the trading days during the three past calendar months
- The company must have at least 2,000 shareholders
- The company must have at least 7,000,000 publicly held shares

If a specific stock fails to meet the qualifications above the options exchanges will not allow any option to be traded for that stock. That's why most of the time you will not see options on penny stocks or stocks that are priced very low.

So what is a stock options chain?

An options chain will show you all of the stock options contracts that are available for a specific stock. Being able to read an options chain is crucial to understanding options. If you don't know how to read an options chain you are essentially flying blind.

An options chain shows the current available call and put strike prices for an underlying stock. They also show the expiration month of the options contract. Reading an options chain can sometimes be confusing because they will slightly vary in layout from broker to broker and from different online sources.

At the end of the day they have the same information. If you are using a free resource such as Yahoo, MSN, CBOE or others, please note that their quotes may be skewed or delayed. If you plan on trading options you can use free resources to get a general idea of how the options are pricing. Once you get ready to put in a trade I would highly suggest using your brokerage platform to get a more precise metric for the options you will trade.

Your brokerage platform will quote you the bid and the ask price in real time and give you more definitive statistics for your options contracts.

The site we will be using to help you understand how to read an options chain is www.barchart.com. They are a fantastic resource to analyze any type of trading instrument. Let's take a look at what an options chain looks like on **Tesla Inc. (TSLA) .**

This is what a typical options chain will look like on call options. Put options will also look the same. Each different part of the options chain that you need to know about has a number in red next to it. Let's go over each one.

Exhibit 1.1

Tesla Inc. (TSLA)-(Calls and Puts)

Tesla Inc. (TSLA) NASDAQ ❶
257.00 +1.01 (+0.39%) 02/24/17
OPTIONS QUOTES for Fri, Feb 24th, 2017

⦿ Set Alerts   ★ Watchlist

Expiration ❹ 2017-03-03 ⌄   Near-the-Money ⌄   Side-by-Side ⌄

			Calls							Puts			
Type	Last	%Chg	Bid	Ask	Volume	Open Interest	Strike	Type	Last	%Chg	Bid	Ask	Volume	Open Interest
Call	24.65	-1.60%	24.05	25.10	8	5	232.50	Put	0.22	-46.34%	0.16	0.23	962	61
Call	21.60	-58.80%	21.65	22.45	12	22	235.00	Put	0.28	-47.17%	0.25	0.32	815	47
Call	16.00	-29.82%	19.25	20.30	3	59	237.50	Put	0.41	-46.75%	0.33	0.43	473	1,05
Call	16.82	-4.38%	16.95	17.70	78	130	240.00	Put	0.55	-48.11%	0.50	0.56	1,739	1,82
Call	15.11	-14.63%	14.75	15.40	11	11	242.50	Put	0.80	-42.86%	0.71	0.85	866	85
Call	12.36	-7.35%	12.60	13.25	55	109	245.00	Put	1.14	-40.00%	1.04	1.20	2,536	1,28
Call	10.40	-2.80%	10.60	11.25	23	77	247.50	Put	1.60	-36.00%	1.48	1.66	854	34
Call	8.70	-3.12%	8.75	9.30	344	803	250.00	Put	2.17	-33.23%	2.10	2.30	4,465	1,90
Call	7.05	-6.00%	7.10	7.55	516	330	252.50	Put	2.95	-27.16%	2.87	3.00	2,733	94
Call	5.92	4.04%	5.60	6.00	1,417	968	255.00	Put	3.90	-27.10%	3.80	4.15	2,102	1,64
Call	4.50	-4.26%	4.35	4.70	1,156	376	257.50	Put	5.30	-19.70%	5.00	5.35	813	428
Call	3.40	-9.33%	3.30	3.60	3,515	1,827	260.00	Put	6.61	-18.40%	6.40	6.80	745	860
Call	2.55	-17.74%	2.46	2.67	972	587	262.50	Put	8.55	-10.09%	8.00	8.45	162	393

1.) This is the name of the company that we are looking at for the options. This will also give you the ticker symbol and the current price of the stock. To the right of the ticker symbol you will see that the option is trading on the NASDAQ .

2.) **"CALLS"** This gives us the type of option pricing we are looking at. In **Exhibit 1.1** we are looking at an option chain for call options and put options stacked side by side.

3.) **"PUTS"** This gives us the options pricing for the put options on Tesla.

4.) **"EXPIRATION"**. This shows us when the options expire. In this case these options expire on 3/3/2017

5.) **"STRIKE"**. This is the different strike prices that are available for trading on the particular stock. The strike price of an option is the price at which the stock can be bought or sold once the option gets exercised.

6.) This column **"LAST"** shows the last price where the options contract was traded. This is the last price at which the transaction took place.

7.) The **"BID"** price is the price that a buyer will pay for that particular stock option. If you are selling stock options this is the price you are willing to receive for the option.

8.) The **"ASK"** price is the price that a seller is willing to accept for that particular option. So if you are planning to buy options, this is the price you want to look at.

9.) The **" %Change "** shows the percent change in the options price since the previous day's closing price.

10.) The **"Volume"** shows how many options contracts have been traded throughout the day

11.) The **"Open Interest"** shows the number of outstanding options contracts. These contracts have not been exercised, closed or expired. If the open interest is high, it means that buying or selling the options contract will be easier because a lot of traders are trading this stock option.

You will see that one section of the options pricing table is lighter and the other section is a darker color. The ones that are lighter are **ITM options**, the other darker section are **OTM options**. You can easily tell this by looking at the current stock price of Tesla which is currently at **$257.00/share.** Any option price below that price will be an ITM option and any price above that will be an OTM option.

This view shows us the call and put options stacked against each other. When it shows them stacked against each other on barchart.com it will not display the implied volatility. Let's take a look at the call options and put options individually so we can see the implied volatility.

Exhibit 1.2

Tesla Inc. (TSLA)-(Call Options Only)

Tesla Inc. (TSLA) NASDAQ
257.00 +1.01 (+0.39%) 02/24/17
OPTIONS QUOTES for Fri, Feb 24th, 2017

Set Alerts   Watchlist

Expiration: 2017-03-03 ⌄   Near-the-Money ⌄   Stacked ⌄

Calls

Strike	Last	% From Last	Bid	Midpoint	Ask	Change	%Chg	IV	Volume	Open Interest
232.50	24.65	+0.10%	24.05	24.58	25.10	-0.40	-1.60%	39.39%	8	5
235.00	21.60	+0.09%	21.65	22.05	22.45	-30.83	-58.80%	33.14%	12	22
237.50	16.00	+0.08%	19.25	19.78	20.30	-6.80	-29.82%	41.39%	3	59
240.00	16.82	+0.07%	16.95	17.33	17.70	-0.77	-4.38%	36.38%	78	130
242.50	15.11	+0.06%	14.75	15.08	15.40	-2.59	-14.63%	39.20%	11	11
245.00	12.36	+0.05%	12.60	12.93	13.25	-0.98	-7.35%	39.59%	55	109
247.50	10.40	+0.04%	10.60	10.93	11.25	-0.30	-2.80%	40.05%	23	77
250.00	8.70	+0.03%	8.75	9.03	9.30	-0.28	-3.12%	39.78%	344	803
252.50	7.05	+0.02%	7.10	7.33	7.55	-0.45	-6.00%	39.75%	516	330
255.00	5.92	+0.01%	5.60	5.80	6.00	0.23	4.04%	39.52%	1,417	968
257.50	4.50	unch	4.35	4.53	4.70	-0.20	-4.26%	39.65%	1,156	376
260.00	3.40	-0.01%	3.30	3.45	3.60	-0.35	-9.33%	39.73%	3,515	1,827
262.50	2.55	-0.02%	2.46	2.57	2.67	-0.55	-17.74%	39.73%	972	587
265.00	1.90	-0.03%	1.79	1.88	1.96	-0.29	-13.24%	39.87%	2,262	825

1.) You can see from the options chain a column that says **"IV"**. This is the implied volatility of the stock. If the implied volatility is very high at a specific strike price compared to the others, the market sentiment is that the price of the stock is likely to gravitate towards that price. This is extremely important to pay attention to.

2.) Here you can see the **"MidPoint"**. This is the midpoint price for the options .This is the difference between the bid and the ask price. This is what you pay or receive for the option. This is crucial when reading an options chain.

This view shows us only the call options on Tesla. It is important to see if a stock has a good options market before we decide to trade it. If a stock does not have a good options market, then there is no point to trade it. It is very important that a stock has a good options market in order for us to successfully trade it. In exhibit 1.3 we can see the put options on Tesla individually.

Exhibit 1.3

Tesla Inc. (TSLA)-(Put Options Only)

Puts

Strike	Last	% From Last	Bid	Midpoint	Ask	Change	%Chg	IV	Volume	Open Interest
232.50	0.22	+0.10%	0.16	0.20	0.23	-0.19	-46.34%	47.62%	962	614
235.00	0.28	+0.09%	0.25	0.29	0.32	-0.25	-47.17%	46.71%	815	479
237.50	0.41	+0.08%	0.33	0.38	0.43	-0.36	-46.75%	44.96%	473	1,057
240.00	0.55	+0.07%	0.50	0.53	0.56	-0.51	-48.11%	43.67%	1,739	1,829
242.50	0.80	+0.06%	0.71	0.78	0.85	-0.60	-42.86%	43.14%	866	853
245.00	1.14	+0.05%	1.04	1.12	1.20	-0.76	-40.00%	42.56%	2,536	1,283
247.50	1.60	+0.04%	1.48	1.57	1.66	-0.90	-36.00%	41.92%	854	342
250.00	2.17	+0.03%	2.10	2.20	2.30	-1.08	-33.23%	41.70%	4,465	1,905
252.50	2.95	+0.02%	2.87	2.94	3.00	-1.10	-27.16%	40.89%	2,733	949
255.00	3.90	+0.01%	3.80	3.98	4.15	-1.45	-27.10%	41.15%	2,102	1,645
257.50	5.30	unch	5.00	5.18	5.35	-1.30	-19.70%	41.05%	813	428
260.00	6.61	-0.01%	6.40	6.60	6.80	-1.49	-18.40%	41.16%	745	860
262.50	8.55	-0.02%	8.00	8.23	8.45	-0.96	-10.09%	41.35%	162	393

What are some of the things that we should look for in good options market for a stock?

- The stock has a high daily volume of shares being traded
- It has good pricing at each available strike price (there is bid and ask price at each strike price)

- Has good volume at each corresponding strike price
- Has open interest at almost every available strike price (does not have to be at every strike price)
- It has great spreads on its options market (Small difference between the bid and ask price)

These are just a few of the factors to consider for a stock options chain in order to decide if we should trade it or not. Tesla is a great example of a stock that has a solid options market. Before you even begin to think about structuring an options trade, look at the current options chain for the stock before making a decision.

The options chain for stock options changes considerably when a stock has an upcoming earnings release. Look for stocks that have upcoming earnings announcements. Stocks will tend to have a robust options market around earnings releases because earnings can cause volatility.

CHAPTER 5: OPTIONS TRADING STRATEGIES

Since we now have a baseline understanding of options, it is now time to get into the fun stuff. There is a plethora of different options trading strategies and there are constantly new ones popping up.

The great thing about options is that it doesn't matter where the stock is trading at. You can always find a great opportunity if you look hard enough. In this chapter we will go over some of the major options trading strategies and some of the more complex ones that allow you to do hedge your risk in very unique ways.

LONG CALL

A long call option is one of the simplest options trading strategies around. You simply buy a long call option if you believe that the price of the underlying security will rise above the strike price.

Long Call Option = Buying 1 ATM Call Option

- **Buy 1 ATM Call Option**

Example

Let's say that US Steel (X) is currently trading at $40/share in January. You look at your options chain and you see that a call options contract with a strike price of $40/share expiring in February is currently priced at $2.

You have reason to believe that US Steel (X) will rise in price by the end of its February expiration and you decide to get into a long call option. For this long call option you pay $200.

Towards the end of the February expiration you are correct and the price of US Steel (X) has gone up to $50/share. You decide to exercise your call option and invoke you right to purchase 100 shares of US Steel (X) at $40 and sell them in the market for $50/share. This yields a nice profit of $10/share.

*Your Net profit on this trade is **$800.***

Appreciation of the long call option = $1,000
Cost to enter the long call option   = $200
*Net Profit on the long call option   = **$800***

If you were wrong and the stock price went down to $30/share your long call option will expire worthless and you only stand to lose the $200 you paid for the option. The great thing about a long call option is that you have fixed risk and unlimited profit potential.

A long call is the most basic type of option you can start off with and they are great to use if you are bullish on a particular stock, but want some sort of fixed risk on the trade.

Below is what a payoff diagram would like for our long call option.

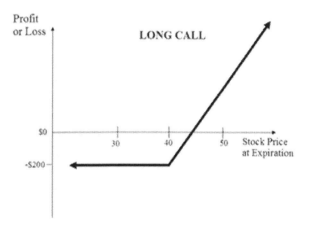

CONCLUSION

A long call option is the easiest way to trade options when you are first starting out. They offer you great leverage when trading a particular stock. You essentially control 100 shares of stock for a fraction of the real price. They can be incredibly profitable when used with a stock that has high implied volatility.

Max Profit Potential *= Unlimited*

Max Loss Potential = *Limited to the price paid for the option + commission costs*

LONG PUT

Like a long call option, a long put option is also another basic options trading strategy that is very simple to use. When you get into a long put option you do it because you have strong reason to believe that the price of the stock will go down.

Long Put Option = Buying 1 ATM Put Option

- **Buy 1 ATM Put Option**

Example

Let's say that US Steel (X) is currently trading at $40/share in January. You look at your options chain and you see that a put options contract with a strike price of $40/share expiring in February is currently priced at $2. You have reason to believe that US Steel (X) will fall in price by the end of its February expiration and you decide to get into a long put option. For this long put option you pay $200.

Towards the end of the February expiration you are correct and the price of US Steel (X) has gone down to $30/share. Your put option is deep in the money with an intrinsic value of $1,000.

*Your net profit on this trade is **$800.***

Intrinsic value of the long put option = $1,000
Cost to enter the long put option   = $200
*Net Profit on the long put option   =**$800***

If you were wrong and the stock price went up to $50/share your long put option will expire worthless and you only stand to lose the $200 you paid for the option. The great thing about a long put option is that you have fixed risk and unlimited profit potential.

A long put option is just the opposite of a long call option. A long call option and long put option both have fixed risk and unlimited profit

potential. Before you get into an options trade, it is important to first
establish some ground work.

- *Time Frame (how long do you want to be in a trade)*
- *Price Range (the price range you expect the stock could possible move)*
- *Risk (how much you plan to risk on the trade)*

Knowing these three parts prior to entering a trade is imperative to managing your trade and being aware of the possible risk that may occur during the life of the trade.

Below is what a payoff diagram would like for our long put option.

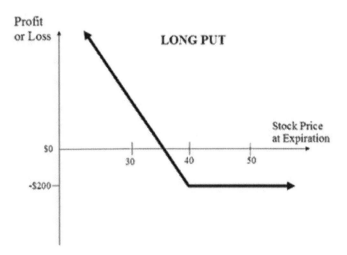

CONCLUSION

A long put option is the easiest way to trade options when you are first starting out. They offer you great leverage when trading a particular stock. If you are bearish a particular stock, a long put option can help you capture profits on a stock when the price begins to fall, while at the same time limiting your downside risk.

Max Profit Potential = Unlimited

Max Loss Potential = *Limited to the price paid for the option + commission costs*

What the heck is OTM (**Out-of-The-Money**) covered call?

An OTM covered call is probably one of my personal favorite options trading strategies. I get so excited talking about covered calls because they are so easy. Let me ask you this. If you owned a house that you were not living in, would you rent it out and make money on it every single month? You would be crazy not to. So why wouldn't you do that with a stock that you own? That's essentially what covered calls are. They are tenants, and you are a landlord.

An OTM covered call is a strategy in which you **sell OTM call options** against the stock that you own.

OTM Covered call = Owning 100 shares of stock + selling 1 OTM call option contract

- ***You own 100 shares of US Steel Corporation (X)***
- ***You sell 1 OTM call option on US Steel Corporation (X)***

With a covered call, you would earn a premium as the seller **(writer)** of the call option and also benefit if your stock appreciates in value depending on how far away your covered call is set. Covered calls have limited earning potential because you essentially give up your right to profit from a serious price move in the stock.

Example

*Let's assume that you own 100 shares of US Steel (X) stock which is trading at $50/share in January. You sell **1 February 55 call for $2**. For this you pay $5,000 for the 100 shares of U.S. Steel (X) and you get $200 for writing the call option. Your total for this is **$4,800**.*

*$5,000 - $200 = **$4,800***

*On expiration in February, the stock has gone to $57. The strike price of $55 is lower than the current market price of $57. The call option is assigned and the writer sells his shares for **$500 profit.***

100 shares x $50/share = $5,000   when first bought the stock
100 shares x $57/share = $5,700   when the option was exercised
Loss of the call premium= $200   premium lost when stock price went above the strike price
*Net Profit on the trade = **$500**   total profit on the trade*

The net profit of $500 is not taking commissions into consideration. Typically they will be small amounts in the $5 to $20 dollar range, but they can vary from broker to broker. Below is what a payoff diagram would like for our OTM covered call trade.

Below is what a payoff diagram would like for our OTM covered call trade.

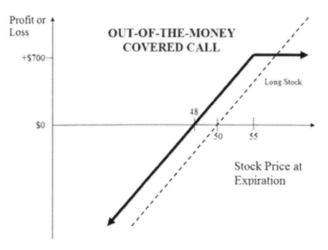

What would it look like if the stock went down $7 instead of up? This would mean that the stock fell to $43 and the call seller (writer) will get hit with a loss of $700 for the shares he is holding. On the other hand he will make $200 in premium for the call option. His total loss would be

$500.

100 shares x $50/share = $5,000   *when he first bought the stock*
100 shares x $43/share= $4,300   *when the option was exercised*
Gain of the call premium= $200   *premium made when the stock stayed*
below the strike price
Net Loss on the trade = $500   *total loss on the trade*

CONCLUSION

OTM covered calls are a great way to make some premium if you believe that the price of a stock will not rally over a certain price point. If you feel that the stock will move up drastically in the next few weeks or and months why not collect some premium on it. It also serves as a mild hedge if the stock does unexpectedly drop down. There are some points to take away from writing covered calls. While they are a great way to collect premium, their profit potential is very limited while having unlimited loss potential.

What you should essentially hope for with writing covered calls is that the price of the stock gets as close to as possible to the strike price of the short call at expiration. This way you can collect your premium at expiration and have some appreciation in the stock. You want the option to expire right at the strike price, this way the profit potential of the trade will be fully maximized.

ITM COVERED CALLS

Buying OTM call options is a great way to maximize your profit potential on stocks that are slowly trending up. But what if you want to protect your stock gains that you have already realized? What if you believe that a stock has ran up too much and is due for a small move to the downside in the next month?

Selling ITM Covered call options is a great way to generate a conservative amount of income with a small amount of risk. ITM covered calls offer downside protection for the stock and can be better than OTM covered calls because the premium earned on ITM covered calls is higher.

An ITM covered call is a strategy in which you **sell ITM call options** against the stock you own

ITM Covered Call = Owning 100 shares of stock +selling 1 ITM call option contract

- *You own 100 shares of US Steel Corporation (X)*
- *You sell 1 ITM call option on US Steel Corporation (X)*

With ITM covered calls your max profit is the premium earned from selling the call option. You won't be able to capture profit from the rise in the price of the stock like you would with OTM call options.

Example

Let's say that US Steel (X) is currently trading at $50 in January. You decide you want to do an ITM covered call. You end up buying 100 shares of US Steel and pay $5,000 and you sell the February $45 call option for $7. You receive $700 in premium for writing the call. Your net investment is $4,300.

*$5,000 - $700= **$4,300***

*On expiration in February, the stock has gone up to $55 and the call option gets assigned. You have to sell your 100 shares of US Steel (X) at the $45 strike price and you end up receiving $4,500 for you shares. You end up profiting **$200** for your trade.*

Total received for shares = $4,500
Total original Investment = $4,300
*Total Net profit   = **$200***

The net profit of $200 is not taking commissions into consideration.

While the ITM covered call is great for protecting your downside, it has limited profit potential. You receive a higher premium for writing an ITM covered call rather than an OTM covered call, but you are limiting yourself to only making money on the premium.

Below is what a payoff diagram would like for our ITM covered call trade.

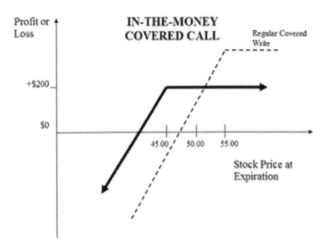

CONCLUSION

ITM covered calls are a better way to protect your downside than writing OTM covered calls. The premium received on them is higher than writing

58

OTM covered calls and can better offset your losses if the price of the stock goes down.

Each one works differently depending on what price range you are targeting. While you have greater downside protection, your maximum loss is unlimited just like it is with OTM covered call.

Your profit with writing ITM covered calls is limited. If the stock begins to appreciate you will not benefit since you have agreed to sell the stock to the buyer at the lower strike price. So your max profit is limited with writing ITM covered calls to the time value of the premium. While these are great ways to generate limited income, they still pose direct unlimited risk.

BULL CALL SPREAD

A bull call spread is an options strategy that is used if you are mildly bullish on a particular stock. It is a great strategy to use if you want fixed risk within in a trade. A bull call spread limits your profit potential on a trade and it also limits how much you can lose. They are great trades if you want to know what your max risk is right off the bat. This strategy is great because you set the trade and you forget it.

A bull call spread is done by buying an ITM (**In-The-Money**) call option and selling (writing) an OTM (**Out-of-The-Money**) call option which has a higher strike price on the same stock within the same expiration month.

BULL CALL SPREAD = Buy 1 ITM Call Option + Sell 1 OTM Call Option

- *Buy 1 ITM Call Option*
- *Sell 1 OTM Call Option*

By getting into a bull call spread you reduce your cost basis for your long call option, but if the stock goes up significantly your profit potential is limited. This is often referred to as a bull call debit spread because there is a net debit associated with placing the trade.

Example

*U.S. Steel (X) is currently trading at $42/share in January and you have reason to believe that it will go up slightly in the next month. You decide to get into a bull call spread by **buying a February 40 call option for $300** and **selling a February 45 call option for $100**. This trade will cost you $200 to get into.*

Buying a February 40 call option = -$300   <<< *cost for buying the call option*

Selling a February 45 call option = $100   <<< *premium received for selling the call option*

Net Cost for this trade = $200   <<< *your net cost for this trade*

The price of U.S. Steel (X) rises and closes to $46/share in the February expiration. Both of the call options expire in-the-money. The February 40 call option has an intrinsic value of $600 and the February 45 call has an intrinsic value of $100. This makes the options trade worth $500. This ends up netting you $300 net profit.

February $40 long call option expires at $46 = +$600
February $45 short call option expires at $46 = - $100
Net Cost for Getting into the call spread   = - $200
Total Net Profit from the call spread   =$+300

The net profit of $300 is not taking commission into consideration.

Below is what a payoff diagram would like for our bull call spread.

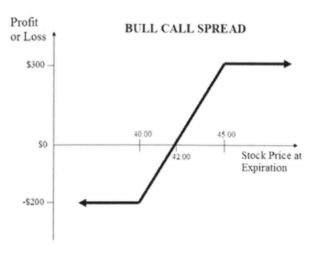

Let's say that stock price had fallen to $38 dollars. If this were the case both of the options would expire worthless. Your max loss would be $200 which is the net cost of the trade. The great thing is that your risk is fixed. You will lose nothing more or nothing less than $200. Bull call spreads are great for investors who want tight risk parameters on their trades and to trade small range bound movements in stocks.

CONCLUSION

Bull call spreads are great ways to trade if you want fixed risk. They eliminate the guesswork and allow you to properly structure your trading setups. By knowing what your maximum loss and profit potential is you can feel comfortable placing a trade. You place bull call spreads to capture a small movement to the upside of the stock and limit your downside if the stock price falls.

It will result in a loss if the stock price falls during expiration. The max loss on a bull call spread will be equal to the debit that is charged to get into the initial trade plus the commissions charged by your broker.

If the stock price is higher than or equal to the strike price of the short call option you reach your max profit potential. So when placing this type of trade you want the stock price to go above the strike price of the short call option or equal to the strike price of the short call option.

Max Profit Potential = Price of the stock > = Strike Price of the Short Call Option

Max Loss Potential = Price of the stock < = Strike Price of the Long Call Option

The bull put spread is an options trading strategy which is used when a trader believes the price of the stocks will go up mildly in the short term. Like the bull call spread, the bull put spread is also used if you want fixed risk. A bull put spread limits your profit potential on a trade and it also limits how much you can lose. It is commonly referred to as a bull put credit spread because you receive a net credit once you enter the trade.

A bull put spread is done by selling an ITM put option with a higher strike price and buying a lower OTM put option on the same stock with the same exact expiration date.

BULL PUT SPREAD = Sell 1 ITM put option + Buy 1 OTM put option

- **Sell 1 ITM Put Option**
- **Buy 1 OTM Put Option**

By getting into a bull put spread you receive a net credit on the trade right off the bat. If the stock prices ends up closing above the higher strike price on expiration, both of the options will expire worthless and you will earn the premium which you took in from entering the trade. Let's have a look at the following example

Example

*U.S. Steel (X) is currently trading at $43/share in January and you have reason to believe that the stock will move up slightly in the next month. You enter into a bull put spread by **buying a February 40 put option for $100** and **selling a February 45 put for $300**. You end up receiving a net credit for $200 dollars for getting into this trade.*

Buying a February 40 put option = -$100   *<<< cost for buying the put option*
Selling a February 45 put option = $300   *<<< premium received for selling the call option*

Net Premium received for trade = $200   <<< net premium received for writing the put option

The price of U.S. Steel (X) rises to $46/share in the February expiration. Both of the options contracts end up expiring worthless and you get to keep the $200 premium as your profit. This is what you want to happen at expiration. The $200 is your max profit potential in this trade.

Let's suppose that the price of the stock had fallen to $38/share in the February expiration .This would mean that both of the options contracts expire ITM with the February 40 put having an intrinsic value of $200 and the February 45 put having an intrinsic value of $700. At expiration this spread is worth $500. The net loss on this trade comes out to $300. The $300 is the max possible loss on this trade. You are risking a max of $300 dollars to make a max of $200.

February 40 put options contract = +$200
February 45 put options contract = -$700
Net Credit received for the spread =+$200
Max Possible Loss on this trade = -$300

This is not taking commission into consideration. Below is what a payoff diagram would like for our bull put spread.

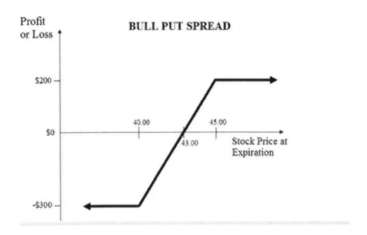

CONCLUSION

Bull put spreads are a great way to trade if you want fixed risk. If you are mildly bullish on a stock this is a good strategy to collect some premium while having fixed risk. If the stock price of the bull put spread falls below the lower strike price on expiration it will result in a max loss that is equal to the difference between the two strike prices of the two put options minus the net credit that is received from the trade.

On the other hand, if the stock prices goes above the higher strike price on expiration, both options will expire worthless and the max you will collect is the premium that you received for writing the put option. Controlled risk and defined profit is what you want in your trading arsenal.

Max Profit Potential = *Price of the stock >= Strike price of the short put option   or just the net premium from writing the call*

Max Loss Potential = *Price of the stock <= Strike price of the long put option*

BEAR CALL SPREAD

The bear call spread is an options trading strategy that is used if you think that the price of the stock will mildly decrease in the short term. This is also commonly referred to as the bear call credit spread because there is a net credit received for getting into the trade. It is also commonly referred to as a vertical spread.

A bear call spread is done by buying call options at a specific strike price and selling an equal number of call options at a lower strike price on the same stock with the same expiration month.

BEAR CALL SPREAD = Buy 1 OTM call option + Sell 1 ITM call option (lower strike price)

- *Buy 1 OTM call option*
- *Sell 1 ITM call option*

By getting into a bear call spread you receive a net credit on the trade right off the bat. The goal of the short call option is to generate income, while the long call options sits as a protective limit. Bear call spreads are great because they have fixed risk. They are great way to trade earnings announcements if you believe that a company will underperform.

Example

*U.S. Steel (X) is currently trading at $37/share in January and you have reason to believe that the stock will go down slightly in the next month. You enter into a bear call spread by **buying a February 40 call for $100** and **selling a February 35 call for $300**. This would give you a net credit of **$200.***

Buying a February 40 call option= -$100   *<<< cost for buying the call option*
Selling a February 35 call option=+$300   *<<< premium received for writing the call option*

Net premium for the spread = **+$200**   <<< *net premium received for the spread*

The price of U.S. Steel (X) falls to $34/share in the February expiration. Both options end up expiring worthless and you get to keep the $200 premium as your profit. The $200 is your max profit potential on this trade.

Let's suppose that the stock went up to $42/share instead. This would mean that both of the call options would expire ITM with the February 40 call having $200 in intrinsic value and the February 35 call having $700 in intrinsic value. This spread would have a net value of $500. This would result in a net loss of $300. The $300 is the max possible loss on this trade.

Net intrinsic value of the trade =   *-$500*
Net Premium received for the spread =   *+$200*
Net Loss on this spread (max) =   **-$300**

This is not taking commission into consideration. Below is what a payoff diagram would like for our bear call spread.

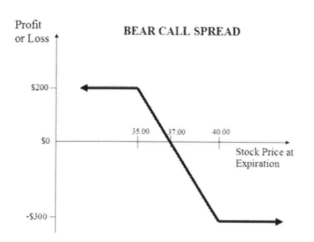

CONCLUSION

Bear call spreads are a great way to trade if you want fixed risk and fixed profit potential. If you are mildly bearish on a particular stock a bear call spread is a great way to collect some premium while minimize the risk of the stock going up.

The max possible gain on bear call spread is limited to the premium earned from getting into the trade. In order for this to happen the price of the stock has to close below the strike price of the lower call when the option expires. This would mean that both of the options contracts would expire worthless. The max possible loss is limited to the difference between the two strike prices on the options minus the credit that was received for getting into the trade. This would mean that the stock price would have to go above the strike price of the higher call option at expiration.

__Max Profit Potential__= Price of the stock <= Strike Price of the short call option, or just the premium received for writing the call

__Max Loss Potential__ = Price of the stock >= Strike Price of the long call option

The bear put spread is an options trading strategy that is used if you think that the price of the stock will mildly decrease in the short term. It is commonly referred to as a vertical spread. It is also referred to as a debit spread because a net debit is charged to get into the trade.

A bear put spread is done by buying an ITM put option and selling an OTM put option on the same stock with the same expiration date.

BEAR PUT SPREAD = Buy 1 ITM put option + Sell 1 OTM put option

- **Buy 1 ITM put option**
- **Sell 1 OTM put option**

By getting into a bear put spread you get charged a net debit right off the bat. Your cost basis is reduced by shorting an OTM put option as you receive a small credit, but you still have a net debit on this trade at the end. This is also another great strategy if you want fixed risk .

Example

*U.S. Steel (X) is currently trading at $38/share in January and you have reason to believe that the stock will go down slightly in the next month. You get into a bear put spread by **buying a February 40 put option for $300** and **selling a February 35 put option for $100**. This costs you $200 to get into the trade.*

Buying a February 40 put option = -$300
Selling a February 35 put option = +$100
*Net Cost to enter the spread   = **$-200***

The price of U.S. Steel (X) falls and closes at $34/share in the February expiration. Both of the put options end up expiring ITM. The February 40 put having $600 in intrinsic value and the February 35 put option having $100 in intrinsic value. This trade would bring in a net profit of $300. This *would be your max possible gain on this trade.*

Value of the February 40 put = +$600
Value of the February 35 put= -$100
Cost to Enter the spread   = -$200
Total Net Profit   = +$300

If the price of the stock had gone up to $42, both of the options would expire worthless and you would lose your $200 debit that you used to get in the trade. This would be you max possible loss on this trade. That's the beauty of getting into spreads, you know what you stand to make or lose if the option expires in your favor or not.

This of course does not take commissions into account. Below is what a payoff diagram would like for a bear put- spread.

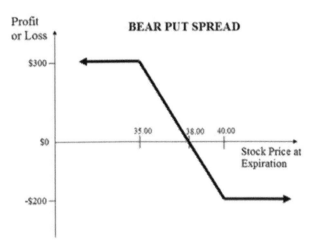

CONCLUSION

Like bear call spreads, bear put spreads are also a great way to trade options if you want defined risk parameters. When you think of spreads, think of fixed risk.

The max possible loss on a bear put spread is limited to the net debit paid to get into the option. They reduce your overall cost basis to get into a trade and also limit your loss if the stock moves up. If the price of the stock goes above the ITM put option strike price at expiration, you only lose the debit amount on the trade. If the stock price closes below the strike price of the OTM put option on the expiration date you will maximize your profit potential on the trade.

***Max Profit Potential**= Price of the stock <= Strike Price of the Short Put Option*

***Max Loss Potential** = Price of the stock >= Strike price of the Long Put Option or the net debit on the trade*

The call back-spread strategy is used if you are bullish a particular stock. This involves selling some call options and at the same time buying more call options so you are net long the stock. It is a strategy which has unlimited upside potential and fixed risk. It is often used with earnings releases when traders are bullish on a stock and believe that it will blow out expectations.

A call back-spread is done by selling 1 ITM call option at a lower strike price and buying twice the amount of long call options at a higher strike price. Whatever number of options you sell, you buy twice that amount for a call back spread.

CALL BACK-SPREAD = Sell 1 ITM call option + Buy 2 OTM call options

- **Sell 1 ITM call option**
- **Buy 2 OTM call options**

When putting on a call back-spread, the trade could result in a net debit, or the cost to get into this could be zero. It depends on the price at that time. Your cost basis is slightly reduced by selling an ITM call option. With this strategy you are expecting the stock to shoot up sharply in the short term and in the off chance that it doesn't you have fixed risk. The upside potential on this type of setup is unlimited while the downside is fixed.

Example

*U.S. Steel (X) is currently trading at $43/share in January and you have reason to believe that the stock will go up after their earnings get released in February. You decide to get into a call back-spread by **selling 1 February 40 call option for $400** and **buying 2 February 45 calls for $200 each.** In this case you pay $0 to get into the trade.*

Selling 1 February 40 call option =+$400   *<<< premium received for writing the call*

72

Buying 2 February 45 call options= -$400   *<<< cost for buying the 2 call options*

Net cost to enter the trade= $0   *<<< net cost to get into this spread*

The price of U.S. Steel (X) explodes to $50/share on earnings in the February expiration and the options end up expiring ITM. The February 40 call is now worth $1,000 and in order to close the position it needs to be bought back.

The two February 45 calls are now worth $500 a piece. This evens out the losses from selling the call option. So if the stock went above $50/share there is no limit to the amount the trader can make after that. The call back-spread will always have a break-even point of some sort. You need to be conscious of what this is prior to getting in the trade.

If the stock had gone to $60/share, the February 45 calls would be worth $1,500 a piece while the short call option would be worth $2,000. This would net you a $1,000 profit. If the stock would have gone to $40 or lower at expiration, the options would expire worthless and you stand to lose only the commission you would have paid to get in this trade.

Below is what a payoff diagram would like for a call back-spread

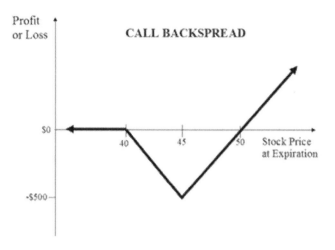

CONCLUSION

The call back-spread is a great options strategy if you want fixed risk and unlimited profit potential. Depending on how the options chain is getting priced out for a particular stock, you can get in this type of trade from little to no cost.

They are great to use during earnings announcements to catch upward movements in the stock. If you plan to deploy this type of strategy I would pay attention to how much the implied volatility of the stock has shifted up in the past week or so. If implied volatility has shifted up by a big percent, the bigger the move in the stock will be once earnings are released.

Max Profit Potential = *Price of the stock – the price of the long call option – Max possible loss (unlimited)*

Max Loss Potential= *Price of the stock = strike price of the long calls (fixed)*

The collar trading strategy is a bit different than other trading strategies because it involves buying the stock, selling a call and buying a put. There is a lot going on here. It is used if you believe that the price of the stock will slowly trend up around a certain price point, but in the off chance that it doesn't you are protected from a drop in the price of the stock. A trader uses this strategy to collect premiums on the covered calls and at the same time have some downside protection from the put option. In order for this to work well, the stock needs to have the right amount of volatility.

The collar is done by buying 100 shares of the underlying stock, selling OTM call options and at the same time buying OTM put options. So it's essentially a covered call along with buying a put option as downside protection.

THE COLLAR = Buy 100 shares of stock + Sell 1 OTM call option + Buy 1 OTM put option

- *Buy 100 shares of stock*
- *Sell 1 OTM call option*
- *Buy 1 OTM put option*

A collar is good strategy if you want fixed risk and fixed profit potential. This is very low risk trading strategy. This can be used for stocks that don't tend to move very much and their trading price is range bound. You should think of a collar as owning a house (**the stock**), renting it out to someone to collect rent (**selling the call**) and having homeowners insurance on it (**buying the put option**).

Example

Let's say that you own 100 shares of Coca-Cola (KO) which is trading at $48/share in January. You decide that the price of the stock will continue *to slowly trend up over the next month and you get into a collar. You **sell the February 40 covered call for $2** and **buy a February 45 put for $1.***

The total cost to enter this trade is $4,700.

Buying 100 shares of Coca-Cola = - $4,800		*<<< 100 shares x 48/share*
Selling the 1 call option for writing the call	*= +$200*	*<<< $2 received*
Buying 1 put option buying the put option	*=- $100*	*<<< cost for*
Total Cost to enter the trade	*= **$4,700***	*<<< total cost to enter the trade*

The price of Coca-Cola (KO) ends up trending to $53/share in the February expiration. The call option gets assigned since the strike price is lower than the trading price and you sell the shares for $5,000. This nets you $300 in profit.

What you sold the shares for = $5,000
Original Trade Cost   = $4,700
*Net Profit on the trade   = **+$300***

Let's say the price of the stock dropped by $5 bucks to $43/share instead. What would the loss look like then? If the stock went to $43/share in the February expiration you would have got hit with a $500 loss for the 100 shares of Coca-Cola (KO). Since you have a put option at the February 45 strike price, you can sell the shares for $4,500 instead of $4,300. So your loss is fixed at $200.

Original cost for the trade = $4,700
What you sell the stock for = $4,500
*Max possible loss   = **$200***

Below is what a payoff diagram would like for a collar

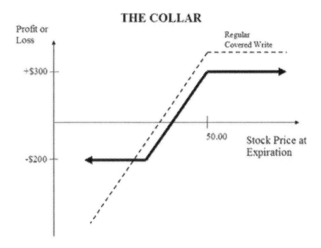

THE COLLAR

CONCLUSION

The collar is a great strategy to use if you believe that a stock will continue to trend up over the next few months. Risk and profit potential are fixed with doing a collar. They are great way to earn a premium if the stock has decent implied volatility and is slowly trending up to a specific price range.

Max Profit Potential = Price of the stock >= Strike price of the short call option

Max Loss Potential = Price of the stock <= Strike price of the long put option

The covered straddle is a strategy that is used if you are bullish on a particular stock. A covered straddle is done by buying 100 shares of stock and selling both calls and puts at the same exact strike price. Another way to think about a covered straddle is a covered call plus a short put option.

It is important to note that this options strategy is not actually fully covered. Only the short call option is covered while the put option is not. This means that this strategy has unlimited risk and fixed profit potential. This strategy is done if you believe that the price of the stock will gravitate up.

COVERED STRADDLE = Buy 100 shares of stock + Sell 1 ATM call option + Sell 1 ATM put option

- ***Buy 100 shares of stock***
- ***Sell 1 ATM call option***
- ***Sell 1 ATM put option***

The call and put options don't have to be ATM. They can be OTM options, but their strike price has to be the same. The negative side to this strategy is that you can experience large losses because the risk is unlimited. You can lose both on the call and put option with this type of strategy. Have a specific price target in mind before getting into this type of trade.

Example

*Let's say that Coca-Cola (KO) is trading at $54/share in January. You are bullish on Coca-Cola (KO) and believe that the stock will go up in the near term. You decide to get into a covered straddle. You end up **buying 100 shares of Coca-Cola (KO) at $54/share, selling 1 February 55 call option for $400 and buying 1 February 55 put option for $300.** The total cost to get in this covered straddle is $4,700.*

Purchasing 100 shares of stock = $5,400   <<< 100 shares x $54/share

Selling 1 February 55 call option = $400   <<< premium received for writing the call

Selling 1 February 55 put option = $300   <<< premium received for writing the put

Net Cost to get in the trade   = **$4,700**   <<< net cost

In the February expiration the stock goes up to $57/share. The February 55 put option expires worthless, but the February 55 call option expires ITM. The 100 shares get sold for $5,500. The total gain on the trade ends up being $800.

Total Premium received on the options = $700
Total value increases in the stock price = $100
Total Net Profit on the covered straddle = **$800**   <<< max possible gain

The $800 is the max possible profit that can be earned on this trade. This amount does not take commission into account.

Let's say the stock price dropped to $45/share in the February expiration instead. In this case the February 55 call option would expire worthless, but the February 55 put option would experience large losses.

The put option has a value of $1,000 and it needs to be bought back at expiration while the stock has lost $900 in value. Your net loss if the trade goes against you is unlimited. In this trade example you would have lost a total of $1,200.

Loss on the short put option = $1,000
Stock value lost   = $900
Premium received for trade = $700
Net Loss on this trade   = **1,200**

(1,000 + 900 − 700) =

Below is what a payoff diagram would like for a covered straddle

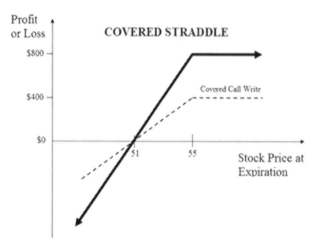

CONCLUSION

Covered straddles are a great trading strategy to use if you have a stock that is not extremely volatile and is on a consistent uptrend. They can be risky because their loss potential is unlimited, while their profit potential is limited.

Max Profit Potential *= Price of the stock > = Strike price of the short call option*

Max Loss Potential *= Unlimited*

The short straddle is a risky trading strategy and should be used with caution. This strategy is used if you believe that the price of the stock will hover around a certain price in the short term. This type of trading strategy is risky because it has unlimited loss potential. A short straddle is done by selling a put option and selling a call option at the same strike price and expiration. It is commonly referred to as naked strangle sale.

SHORT STRADDLE = Selling 1 ATM Call Option + Selling 1 ATM Put Option

- **Sell 1 ATM Call Option**
- **Sell 1 ATM Put Option**

A short straddle is limited in profit and poses an unlimited amount of risk. They should be used if you believe that the stock will experience minimal volatility in the short term.

Example

*Let's say that Coca-Cola (KO) is trading at $40/share in January. You believe that the price will move up in the next month and you get into a short straddle. You end up **selling a February 40 put option for $200** and **selling a February 40 call option for $200.** You end up receiving a $400 credit for this trade since you are writing two options.*

Selling 1 February 40 call option = $200   *<<< premium received for writing the call*

Selling 1 February 40 put option = $200   *<<< premium received for writing the put*

*Net premium received for trade = **$400***

In the February expiration the stock goes up to $50/share. This would make the February 40 put option expire worthless, while the February 40 *call option expire ITM with an intrinsic value of $1,000. This would warrant you a $600 loss.*

Intrinsic value = $1,000
Net Credit   = $400
Net Loss   =$600

If the price of Coca-Cola (KO) stayed around $40 and ended up expiring at $40/share in the February expiration both of the options would expire worthless and you would get to keep your $400 credit from entering the trade. This is also you max possible gain on the trade.

Below is what a payoff diagram would like for a short straddle.

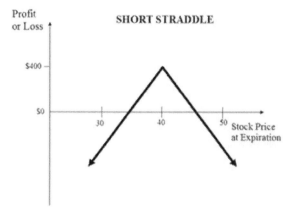

CONCLUSION

The thing about a short straddle is that your max gain is limited to the amount of premium you take in from writing the two options, while your max loss is unlimited.

If the stock happens to move strongly in either direction your options can expire very deep in the money and cause you to incur large losses.

You should look for stocks that don't tend to move very much and have a low beta if you want to deploy this strategy

Max Profit Potential= *Price of the stock = Strike price the two options*

Max Loss Potential= *Unlimited*

The long straddle is another great options trading strategy. It functions just like a short straddle but in the opposite direction. This is done by buying a put option and buying a call option on the same stock, same strike price and same expiration date.

LONG STRADDLE = Buying 1 ATM Call Option + Buying 1 ATM Put Option

- ***Buy 1 ATM Call Option***
- ***Buy 1 ATM Put Option***

Long straddles are slightly different than short straddles because they have fixed risk and unlimited profit potential. These are done if you have reason to believe that a stock will go up significantly in the short term.

This is a good way to trade earnings announcements if you have a strong biased that a company will perform better than expected. These are great to deploy during news announcements because you have defined risk and unlimited profit potential.

Example

Let's say that Coca-Cola (KO) is trading at $40/share in January. The stock has an earnings announcement scheduled January 23 and you have reason to believe that the stock will outperform Wall Street estimates and rise up sharply after earnings are released.

*You get into a long straddle by **buying 1 January 40 put option for $200** and **buying a 1 January 40 call option for $200.** You get charged a net debit of $400 for this trade. This $400 net debit charged on this trade is your max possible loss.*

Earnings get released on January 23 and Coca-Cola (KO) blows through Wall Street estimates and the stock goes up to $50/share in the January expiration. The January 40 put option expires worthless, while the January

40 call option expires ITM. The intrinsic value on this trade is $1,000 and the net profit comes out to $600.

Intrinsic Value of the January 40 call option = $1,000
Initial cost to get into the long straddle   = $400
Net Profit on the long straddle   = $600

If the price of Coca-Cola (KO) had stayed at $40/share and didn't move during the January expiration, you would be limited to $400 as the max possible loss. This is the initial amount you paid to get in the long straddle. This amount is not taking commissions into account.

This is a great strategy around news because your risk is fixed and your profit is unlimited.

Below is what a payoff diagram would like for a long straddle.

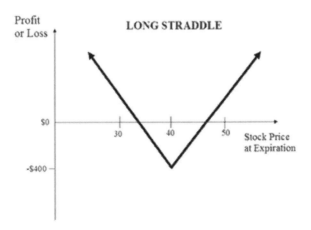

CONCLUSION

The great thing about a long straddle is that you have unlimited profit potential while having defined risk. They are a function of volatility and they function best when the price of a stock moves up significantly. Stocks that have high betas are good to trade with this kind of strategy.

Max Profit Potential= _Unlimited_

Max Loss Potential = _Net Debit charged to get into the straddle_

The short strangle is a trading strategy which can be pretty risky because it has limited profit potential and unlimited risk. This strategy is done if you believe that a stock will have small volatility in the short term. They are commonly referred to as credit spreads because you receive a net credit to enter into the trade. They are done by selling an OTM call option and an OTM put option on the same stock and the same expiration.

SHORT STRANGLE = Selling 1 OTM Call Option + Selling 1 OTM Put Option

- ***Sell 1 OTM Call Option***
- ***Sell 1 OTM Put Option***

If you have reason to believe that a certain stock will stay about the same price in the short term you can enter into a short strangle and collect some premium. A short strangle is good to use for low volatility stocks that tend to consolidate around a certain price point.

Example

*Let's say that Microsoft (MSFT) is trading at $40/share in January. You decide that the price will stay around $40/share and not move in the next month. You get into a short strangle **by selling a February 35 put option for $100** and **selling a February 45 call option for $100**. You receive a net credit of $200 for this transaction*

In the February expiration, Microsoft (MSFT) ends up rallying to $50/share. The February 35 put option will expire worthless in this case, while the February 45 call option will expire ITM with an intrinsic value of $500. Your net loss in this trade comes out $300.

Value of the call option on expiration = $500
Value of the put option on expiration =$200
*Net loss writing the short strangle = **$-300***

Let's say that the price of Microsoft (MSFT) stayed at $40/share in the February expiration. If this happened the February 35 put option and the February 45 call option would expire worthless and you would get to keep your credit of $200 that you originally received to enter this trade.

The short strangle is great if you have strong reason to believe that the price of a stock will stay around a certain price point and won't deviate too much from it. They are a good way to collect premium on non-momentum stocks with low betas.

The thing to note about short strangles is that they have unlimited risk and should be used with caution. There really isn't a limit as to how much you can lose with them.

The main thing to look at when deciding to enter into a short strangle is seeing the range that the stock has been trading in for the past 3 months and seeing if there are any external factors that might push in beyond those ranges. Identify the range and structure your trade around those ranges.

Below is what a payoff diagram would like for a short strangle

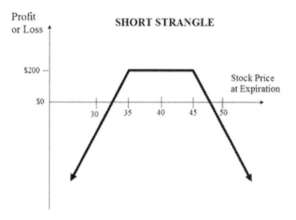

CONCLUSION

Short strangles can lead to large losses if the price of the stock moves sharply out of the set ranges in the trade. They can be a great way to capture some premium if the price of the stock is in consolidation or minimal movement.

Max Profit Potential= *Limited to the amount of credit received when entering into the trade*

Max Loss Potential = *Unlimited*

LONG STRANGLE

The long strangle is an options trading strategy which is done if you believe the price of a stock will experience a strong move to the upside within a short period of time. It involves buying OTM call options and buying OTM put options on the same stock with the same expiration date.

LONG STRANGLE = Buying 1 OTM Call Option + Buying 1 OTM Put Option

- ***Buy 1 OTM Call Option***
- ***Buy 1 OTM Put Option***

This options strategy looks to capture price increases in the implied volatility of the stock. Stocks with high implied volatility will tend to generate the most return for this type of trade setup. The great thing about this strategy is that the max loss is limited, while the profit is unlimited.

Example

*Let's say that Microsoft (MSFT) is trading at $40/share in January. You have reason to believe that the price will skyrocket in the next month. You decide to get into a long strangle by buying a **February 35 put option for $100** and a **February 45 call option for $100**. You are charged $200 debit to get into this trade.*

At the February expiration Microsoft (MSFT) rallies to $50/share. This would mean that the February 35 put option will expire worthless, while the February 45 call option expires ITM. The intrinsic value of the call option is $500. The net profit for this would be $300.

Intrinsic value of the call option at expiration = $500
Net Debit to enter the long strangle   = $200
*Net Profit on the long strangle   = **$300***

Let's say that the price of Microsoft (MSFT) ended up at $40/share in the February expiration. This would mean that the February 35 put option and the February 45 call option would both expire worthless. Your max loss on this trade is limited to your $200 debit that was used to enter the trade.

That's the beauty of a long strangle. You have fixed risk parameters and unlimited profit potential. The max gain on this type of trade occurs if the price of the stock goes to infinity. If implied volatility increases while you are in this trade it can have a very positive effect on the trade. It can help push the value of the options higher and you can close your trade out prior to expiration.

It's important to note that you can exercise your option prior to expiration. If you are deep in the money with a long strangle you can take your profits early and exercise the option prior to expiration.

With a long strangle you are essentially buying volatility and expecting that volatility will increase over the life of the option. The two main factors at play with this strategy are time decay and volatility.

Time decay is constant and decreases the value of the position little by little every day. So if a long strangle goes deep in the money early on in the options life, it can be good to exercise that option earlier as well. Sometimes you need to take profits earlier on and exercise your option. It can prove to be more profitable than just sitting there waiting until expiration.

Below is what a payoff diagram would like for a long strangle

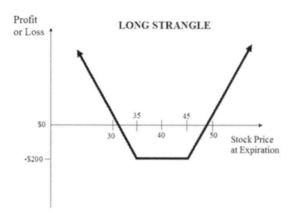

CONCLUSION

A long strangle is a great strategy to use if you want defined risk and unlimited profit potential. With this strategy you are hoping that the implied volatility goes up throughout the life of the option.

If the price of the stock sends your option deep in the money, you can exercise the option prior to the expiration date. By exercising your option earlier on in the options life, you are decreasing your time decay risk. This is best done if the price of the stock moves very sharply in your favor in the short term.

Max Profit Potential*= Unlimited*

Max Loss Potential*= Limited to the net premium paid to enter the strangle*

The married put is an options trading strategy that is used when you are bullish on a particular stock. It is commonly used if you already own shares of a particular stock as a way to protect your downside. With a married put you buy an ATM put option and at the same time you buy 100 shares of the stock. You go in this trade knowing your max possible gain, while your upside potential is unlimited.

MARRIED PUT = Buying 1 ATM Put Option + Buying 100 shares of stock

- **Buy 1 ATM Put Option**
- **Buy 100 shares of stock**

The married put is attractive to traders because it offers fixed risk and unlimited profit potential. It looks for price increases in the stock in the short term. A married put is often referred to as a synthetic long call option.

Example

You are bullish on IBM stock but are unsure of future short term performance. You decide to enter into a married put option.

You buy 100 shares of stock trading at $52/share in January and buy the February 50 put option for $2 *to protect your purchase of the 100 shares of stock. Your total cost to enter this trade is* **$5,400**.

Buying the 100 shares of stock at $52/share = $5,200
Buying the put option for $2   = $200
Total cost to enter the trade   = $5,400

The great thing about a married put is that you have unlimited profit potential. Let's say that the price of the stock goes to $80/share. Your *profit will be $28/share minus the $2 paid for the put protection. So a total gain of $26/share.*

Suppose the price of the stock goes against you and dives below $50/share at expiration. Since you have a protective put in place at $50/share, even if the price of the stock goes to $30/share you are only limited to a max loss of $4/share.

Loss on the put option   = $2/share
Depreciation on the stock = $2/share
Total Max Loss   = $4/share

The other scenario with a married put is that the price of the stock remains unchanged and stays at $52/share. In this case you stand to lose just the $2/share you paid in premium for the put option.

This is great if you want temporary protection on a stock that you own. This can be best thought of as having a small insurance policy on your stock.

Below is what a payoff diagram would like for a married put.

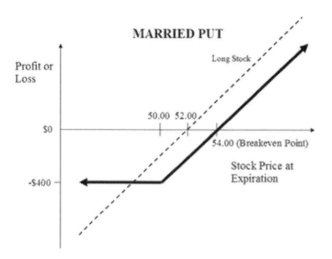

CONCLUSION

A married put is a great trading strategy if you are bullish on a particular stock, but want some downside protection at a level that you feel comfortable selling the stock at. It's a great way to protect long term investment gains from sharp declines in the short term.

Max Profit Potential = *Unlimited*

Max Loss Potential = *Limited to the premium paid to enter the put option + the amount of stock depreciation at the put option strike price*

COVERED COMBO

The covered combo is an options trading strategy that is used if an investor is mildly bullish on a particular stock. It is commonly used by investors who are looking for additional sources of premium income.

A covered combo options strategy is done by buying 100 shares of stock, selling OTM call options and selling OTM put options at the same strike price and expiration date.

COVERED COMBO = Buying 100 shares of stock + Selling 1 OTM Call Option + Selling 1 OTM Put Option

- **Buy 100 shares of stock**
- **Sell 1 OTM Call Option**
- **Sell 1 OTM Put Option**

It is important to note that you can experience significant losses with this strategy if the price of the stock moves down sharply at expiration. The reason it is so high risk is because it can lose money on the put option, call option and from depreciation in the stock.

Example

Let's assume that IBM is currently trading at $52/share in January. You are mildly bullish on IBM and decide to enter into a covered combo.

*You buy 100 shares of stock trading at $52/share in January and at the same time **sell a February 50 put option for $100** and **sell a February 55 call option for $100**.*

*The total cost to enter the covered combo is **$5,000**.*

Purchasing 100 shares at $52/share = $5,200
Premium received for the put option = $100
Premium received for the call option = $100
*Net Cost to enter the trade   = **$5,000***

On expiration in February, IBM goes above the strike price to $57/share. The February 50 put option ends up expiring worthless, while the February 55 call option expires in the money. Your 100 shares get called away for $5,500 and you make a $300 dollar gain on the stock position.

Your net profit ends up being $500. This is you max possible profit on this trade.

Gain on the long stock position = $300
Premium received for the trade = $200
Net Profit on this trade   = **$500**

Let's see how this type of trade can go bad if it goes strongly against you. Let's assume you were wrong and the price of the stock dropped to $45/share in the February expiration. If this happened your February 55 call option would expire worthless while your February 50 put option and stock position suffer significant losses.

The February 50 put option is now worth $500 and has to be bought back while at the same time the stock position has lost $700 in value. You have your $200 you received in premium for entering this trade. Your total loss in this scenario comes out to **$1,000**.

Value lost from stock position	= $700
Loss from the put option	= $500
Premium earned from entering trade	= $200
Total Loss on this trade	=**$1,000**

Below is what a payoff diagram would like for a covered combo.

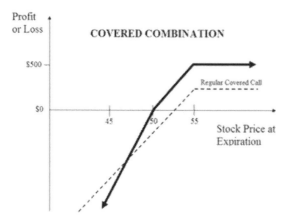

CONCLUSION

It is imperative to be extremely careful when entering into a covered combo. While they are good for short term gains, they can present massive drawdowns since their risk is virtually unlimited. If you decide to get into this type of trade, don't do it around major news releases such as earnings announcements. It is meant to be used in low volatility conditions.

Max Profit Potential *= Limited*

Max Loss Potential *= Unlimited*

The uncovered put write is an options trading strategy that is used to capture income by collecting premiums. It is accomplished by simply selling a put option at the money. It is also commonly referred to as naked put. You get into this type of trade if you are bullish a stock and want to collect premiums.

UNCOVERED PUT WRITE = Sell 1 ATM Put Option

- ***Sell 1 ATM Put Option***

The primary goal of this strategy is to earn consistent premium income. It is meant to identify low risk opportunities that will help you capture small chunks of premium over and over again. As an uncovered put writer, you sell slightly OTM put options each month and collect small amounts of premium.

Example

*Let's assume that IBM is currently trading at $45/share in January. You are mildly bullish on IBM and decide to enter into an uncovered put. **You sell a February 45 put option for $200.***

On expiration in February, IBM goes above the strike price to $50/share. Your February 45 put option expires worthless and you get to keep your $200 in premium that you received for writing the put option. With this type of trade your profit is limited to your premium amount.

*Let's assume you were wrong and the price of IBM went down to $40 in the February expiration. If this was the case the February 45 put option would expire ITM with $500 in intrinsic value. This means that the put option needs to be bought back for $500. This would result in a net loss of **$300.***

Intrinsic Value of the put option   = $500

Net premium for writing put option   = $200
Net loss on this trade   **=$300**

This strategy can be good if you find a slowly trending stock that doesn't tend to have massive swings in price. You can capture small and consistent profits. It is important to note that his strategy can have some serious downside risk if the positions aren't properly managed.

If the price of the stock drops too quick you can lose a hefty amount. Your maximum loss is virtually unlimited while your max profit is limited to the premium earned for writing the put option. To avoid large losses with this strategy, you can shift out your put option further OTM.

TRADE SHIFTING

By slightly adjusting the trade if it happens to move against you, you are in a way limiting your max potential loss. You don't want to overextend your option OTM too much because the premium you earn will be reduced. If you begin to get into a losing position, look at the options chain and see if there are any plausible options available to shift your trade further OTM.

This will involve you exercising your option and taking a small loss and immediately opening one with the same contract month you did before, but further OTM. You are simply closing your position and opening another one that is further OTM.

That is what separates options trading from everything else. They are extremely flexible and dynamic. If you are caught in a losing position you can essentially adjust your trade out of a loss if you know the proper combination of spreads to deploy. If you see that you are in a losing position there is no need to panic, there is simply a need to adjust.

You can hedge your position by creating a different spread. If the put option goes against you, you can buy a put option to hedge your current loss at a strike price that is reasonable. If you decide to do this, be aware that buying a put will cost you money, but it can limit your losses.

Below is what a payoff diagram would like for an uncovered put write.

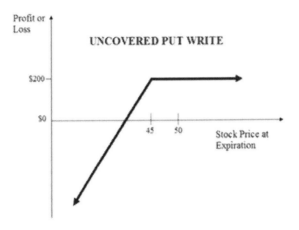

CONCLUSION

Naked put options can be a great way to capture small profits with slow moving stocks that don't tend to move very much. While they can be a great way to generate income, they can carry unlimited risk if not correctly adjusted.

Max Profit Potential= Limited to the premium earned for writing the put

Max Loss Potential= Unlimited

CHAPTER 6: ADVANCED STRATEGIES

Before moving to this section, it is imperative that you master the basic strategies first. If you don't know the difference between each spread and strangle, the advanced strategies are going to confuse you and leave you lost.

The following strategies discussed in this chapter are used by elite traders. These strategies can make you into a master trader if you apply yourself and fully understand how they work. By mastering the advanced strategies and all their little intricacies you will become a consistently profitable trader and be on your way to becoming a millionaire.

Let's begin !!!

✓ THE STOCK REPAIR STRATEGY

The stock repair strategy is meant to be used if you have bought shares of stock in a company at a price above the current market price and you want to minimize your losses and hopefully break-even on the trade.

The main goal of this strategy is to recover from a losing position after a long stock position has incurred losses. This strategy does not protect you from incurring additional downside loss, but it also doesn't increase the probability of you incurring losses on the downside either. It simply reduces your break- even point.

The stock repair strategy involves buying 1 ATM call option and selling 2 OTM call options. It can typically be referred to as a call ratio spread. This can be built many different ways, but the option below is standard. Remember that this is done on top of owning 100 shares of stock or more. *STOCK REPAIR STRATEGY = Buying 1 ATM call option + Selling 2 OTM call options*

(on top of your original stock position depending how big it is, for this example we will assume 100 shares of stock)

- *Buy 1 ATM Call Option*
- *Sell 2 OTM Call Options*

A common way to reduce your break-even price is to double down and buy twice as many shares to reduce the average purchase price. This will reduce your break-even price, but you will have to add additional money to your position. This can be risky if the stock price continues on a downward spiral.

By using options to repair a losing stock position you don't have to pump in any additional funds and can be virtually cost free. This strategy can actually be set up to have you making money once the options expire. This strategy is mostly used to break-even and reduce your overall cost basis in a losing position.

Example

Let's assume that you have **purchased 100 shares of IBM at $50/share** in January. A month later the price has fallen to $40/share with a potential loss of $1,000. You don't want to take a loss on this position and decide that you will use the stock repair strategy to reduce your break-even price.

You end up **buying a March 40 call option for $200** and **selling 2 March 45 call options for $100/each**. The cost for you to enter this trade is $0.

Cost to purchase the March 40 call option   = -$200
Premium received for selling 2 March 45 call options = +$200
Total Cost to enter this trade   = $0

In the March expiration IBM is trading at $45/share. This would mean that both of the March 45 call options would expire worthless while the March 40 call option would expire ITM with an intrinsic value of $500.

If you chose to exercise your long call option, it would yield you a profit of $500. The long stock position would have earned back $500 in value. The total gain comes out to $1,000.

The $1,000 you gained from doing the stock repair strategy ends up getting you to break even from your original $1,000 loss on the long stock position.

If IBM went the other way and made its way to $60/share in the March expiration, all of the call options would expire ITM, but you have sold more call options than you have bought, so you will need to buy back the written call options at a loss.

Each of the March 45 call options are now valued at $1,500, but the long March 40 call option is only worth $2,000 and it's not enough to cover the losses from the written call options.

This means that you have incurred a loss of $1,000 from the trade, but this loss is actually offset by the $2,000 gain from the long stock position. This yields a profit of $1,000. This is the amount of the initial loss on the long stock positions.

Initial Long Stock Positions Loss   = -$1,000
Value of the 2 March 45 call options   = $3,000 ($1,500 x 2)

Value of the long March 45 call option = $2,000

Gain on the Long stock Position   = $2,000
Net Profit from entering the repair strategy $0 << break even

So, with the stock price reaching $60 with this strategy you would repair your trade and end up breaking even. The thing about this strategy is you can only break even, but your downside risk is essentially fixed.

You can actually make money with this trade if you sold more call options and bought more stock to reduce your break-even price further down and actually earn more premium. This can however carry some significant risk.

Below is what a payoff diagram would like our stock repair strategy.

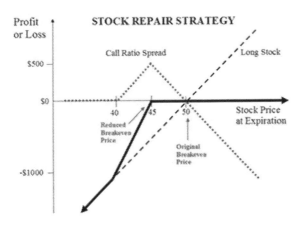

CONCLUSION

There is no need to panic if you begin to get into a losing stock position. There are different combinations and strategies to repair your position and come out at break-even. Options are extremely flexible and can provide you with unique strategies to lower your risk and maximize your profit potential.

The stock repair strategy can be structured in many different ways to help you break even on a losing position. With the strategy we described there is no additional downside risk and you can't make a significant profit you're your break –even price unless you sell more call options. This is a strategy that is to be used to reduce your losses and cushion the risk of a stock move to the downside.

LONG CALL BUTTERFLY

What is a long call butterfly?

A long call butterfly is an options trading strategy that is done if you have reason to believe the price of the stock will not fall or rise much by the expiration date. The long call butterfly is a fixed risk trading strategy. It involves 3 different options contracts. It will result in a net debit trade.

LONG CALL BUTTERFLY = Buying 1 ITM Call Option + Selling 2 ATM Call Options + Buying 1 OTM Call Option

- *Buy 1 ITM Call Option   (wing 1)*
- *Sell 2 ATM Call Options*
- *Buy 1 OTM Call Option   (wing 2)*

IMPORTANT FACTS TO KNOW ABOUT BUTTERFLY SPREADS

- *The best way to visually interpret butterfly spreads is by actually thinking of the two outer options as wings of a butterfly.*

- *Try to actually picture the option as a butterfly. The head of the butterfly will have 2 options while the wings each have one option. One wing will be an ITM option and another will be an OTM option.*

- *Majority of the time when doing a butterfly spread, the middle (head of the butterfly) option will typically be an ATM option. This is majority of the time, but not 100% of the time. You can structure it slightly different to where the head of the option is slightly ITM or slightly OTM.*

- *When putting together a butterfly spread, the wings of the options should be the same distance in price from the middle option. If the strike price of your middle option is $20, your wings should be $25 and $15. The outside wings are both $5 away from the middle strike price of $20. If one wing was $5 dollars away from your middle strike price and another wing was only $2 dollars away you, are shifting your trade towards being more long or short biased. Keep the wings proportional to one another.*

- *This is important to remember because if your distance from 1 wing changes without proportion to the other you are creating a heavier biased towards the direction of the stock.*

- *Your risk of losing is limited as well as your potential profit.*

Example

*Let's say that Microsoft (MSFT) is trading at $40/share in January. You have reason to believe that the price will not move much by the February expiration and you decide to enter into a long call butterfly. **You end up buying a February 30 call option for $1,100, selling 2 February 40 call options for $400 per piece and buying a February 50 call option for $100.** This will result in a net debit for the trade.*

Our Trade

- Buying a February 30 Call Option = -$1,100
- Selling 2 February 40 Call Options= +$800 ($400 x 2)
- Buying a February 50 Call Option = +100
- **Net Debit = -$400**

Let's assume that the price of Microsoft (MSFT) is still trading around $40/share in the February expiration. If this was the case the February 40 call option and the February 50 call option would expire worthless. The

February 30 call option would have an intrinsic value of $1,000. Taking out the initial debit of $400 that charged for getting into the trade, you have a max possible profit of $600 for this trade.

*Now let's assume that the price of Microsoft (MSFT) is trading **below $30** or **above $50** in the February expiration. If this was the case the max possible loss is limited to the initial debit on the trade. It would be limited to the initial $400 that was used to enter the trade. For this trade you are essentially risking $400 dollars to make $600. This is a solid payoff with limited risk.*

The long call butterfly is great to use for a stock that doesn't see too much volatility and stays within a certain range of price. If the trade happens to go against you and goes through your set price ranges it is okay because with this strategy you have fixed risk.

You know how much you stand to lose prior to even getting in the trade, so there aren't any surprises when the trade happens to move against you. You have upside and downside protection.

Below is what a payoff diagram would like for a long call butterfly

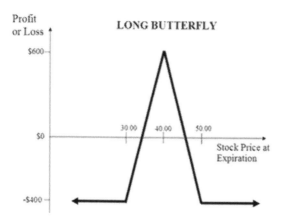

CONCLUSION

The long call butterfly is a great strategy to use if you believe that the price of the stock will have limited price movements in the short term. For this type of strategy to work you need to focus on finding stocks that have low volatility. This is a great strategy to use because it has fixed risk.

When searching for options to use this strategy on you need to focus on having a much higher payout than possible loss. You should focus on having a payout that is approximately 20%-50% higher than the max possible loss. In our example we risked $400 to make $600. When you structure your trades to have fixed risk and a positive payout ratio, over time you will be consistently profitable.

With our trade example if you had a 50% win ratio, you would still be profitable.

- Trade win = +600
- Trade Loss= -400
- Trade Win = +600
- Trade Loss = -400
- **Total Net profit = +$400**

***Max Profit Potential**= Limited*

***Max Loss Potential**= Limited to the net debit of the trade*

What is a short call butterfly?

A short call butterfly is an options trading strategy that is done if you are neutral on the direction of a stock but bullish on the volatility of the stock. In this case you don't really care in which direction the stock moves, you just want the price to move. The short call butterfly is a fixed risk trading strategy. It involves 3 different options contracts. It will results in a net credit trade.

SHORT CALL BUTTERFLY = Sell 1 ITM Call Option + Buy 2 ATM Call Options + Sell 1 OTM Call Option

- **Sell 1 ITM Call Option   (wing 1)**
- **Buy 2 ATM Call Options**
- **Sell 1 OTM Call Option (wing 2)**

Our short call butterfly consist of two long call options at the middle strike price and short one call option at each upper and lower strike price. The two short call options must be the same distance from the middle strike price.

Example

*Let's say that Microsoft (MSFT) is trading at $40/share in January. You decide to get into a short call butterfly. You end up **selling a February 30 call option for $1,100, buying two February 40 call options for $400 each** and **selling one February 50 call option for $100**. For this transaction you take in a net credit of $400. The net credit taken in for a short call butterfly is the max profit.*

Our Trade

- Selling a February 30 Call Option = +$1,100
- Buying 2 February 40 Call Options= -$800 ($400 x 2)

- Selling a February 50 Call Option = +100
- **Net Premium Received = + $400**

Let's assume that the price of Microsoft (MSFT) has dropped to $30/share in the February expiration. If this was the case, all the call options would expire worthless. You would get to keep your net credit of $400 that was originally taken in to set up the short call butterfly. This is your max possible profit for this trade.

Let's assume that the price of Microsoft (MSFT) ends up staying around $40/share in the February expiration. If this was the case, all except the lower strike call option would expire worthless. The lower strike call option would now have a value of $1,000 and has to be bought back. Taking out the initial credit of $400 that was received for getting into the trade, you have a max possible loss of $600 for this trade.

You want the price of the stock to move in either direction. If the stock ends up staying around the middle strike at expiration you will incur a loss. The profit and loss are limited in a short call butterfly which is good because you know your risk before ever getting into the trade.

Below is what a payoff diagram would like for a short call butterfly

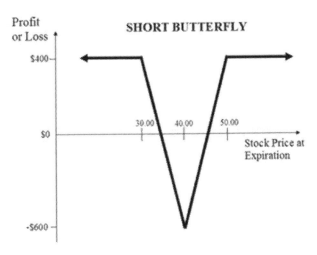

CONCLUSION

The short call butterfly is a great strategy to use if you are neutral on the direction of a stock, but bullish on the volatility of the stock. The strategy is great to use because it has fixed risk. You know your risk before you get into the trade and are protected from any nasty moves.

Max Profit Potential= *Limited to the net premium earned on the trade*

Max Loss Potential= *Limited*

Like the short call butterfly, the short put butterfly is also an options trading strategy that is neutral on the direction of a stock but bullish on the volatility of the stock. The only difference here is that the short put butterfly uses put options instead of call options. The short call butterfly is a fixed risk trading strategy. It involves 3 different options contracts.

SHORT PUT BUTTERFLY = Selling 1 ITM Put Option + Buy 2 ATM Put Options + Sell 1 OTM Put Option

- ***Sell 1 ITM Put Option   (wing 1)***
- ***Buy 2 ATM Put Options***
- ***Sell 1 OTM Put Option   (wing 2)***

Our short put butterfly consist of two put options at the middle strike price and short one put option at each upper and lower strike price. The two short put options must be the same distance from the middle strike price.

Example

*Let's say that Microsoft (MSFT) is trading at $40/share in January. You decide to get into a short put butterfly. You end up **selling a February 30 put option for $100, buying two February 40 put options for $400 each** and **selling another February 50 put option for $1,100**. For this transaction you take in a net credit of $400. The net credit taken in for a short call butterfly is the max profit.*

Our Trade

- Selling a February 30 Put Option = +$100
- Buying 2 February 40 Put Option = -$800 ($400 x 2)
- Selling a February 50 Put Option = +$1,100
- **Net Premium Received = + $400**

Let's assume that the price of Microsoft (MSFT) has dropped to $30/share in the February expiration. If this was the case, all the put options would expire worthless. You would get to keep your net credit of $400 that was originally taken in to set up the short put butterfly. This is your max possible profit for this trade.

Let's assume that the price of Microsoft (MSFT) ends up staying around $40/share in the February expiration. If this was the case, all except the higher strike put option would expire worthless. The lower strike price put option would now have a value of $1,000 and has to be bought back. Taking out the initial credit of $400 that was received for getting into the trade, you have a max possible loss of $600 for this trade.

Like the short call butterfly, you don't care in which direction your short put butterfly moves, you just want it to move. If the stock ends up staying around the middle strike at expiration you will incur a loss. The profit and loss are limited in a short put butterfly which is good because you know your risk before ever getting into the trade. Limited risk options strategies will preserve your capital and help you slowly grow your account over time.

Below is what a payoff diagram would like for a short put butterfly

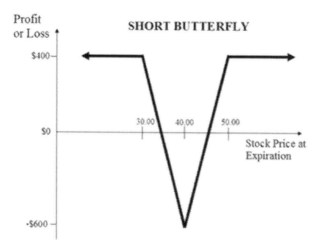

CONCLUSION

The short put butterfly is a great strategy to use if you are neutral on the direction of a stock, but bullish on the volatility of the stock. The strategy is great to use because it has fixed risk. You know your risk before you get into the trade and are protected from any nasty moves.

Max Profit Potential*= Limited to the net premium earned on the trade*

Max Loss Potential*= Limited*

The long put butterfly is an options trading strategy that is done when you believe the price of the stock won't move much by the expiration date. The long put butterfly is a fixed risk trading strategy. Like the short put butterfly, it also involves 3 different options contracts.

LONG PUT BUTTERFLY = Buying 1 OTM Put Option + Selling 2 ATM Put Options + Buying 1 ITM Put Option

- *Buy 1 OTM Put Option (wing 1)*
- *Sell 2 ATM Put Options*
- *Buy 1 ITM Put Option (wing 1)*

Our long put butterfly consist of two put options at the middle strike price and long one put option at each upper and lower strike price. The two long put options must be the same distance from the middle strike price.

Example

*Let's say that Microsoft (MSFT) is trading at $40/share in January. You don't think that the price will move much by the February expiration and you decide to get into a long put butterfly. You end up **buying a February 30 put option for $100, selling 2 February 40 put options for $400 each** and **buying a February 50 put option for $1,100**.*

Our Trade

- Buying a February 30 Put Option = -$100
- Selling 2 February 40 Put Options = +$800 ($400 x 2)
- Buying a February 50 Put Option = -$1,100
- **Net Debit = -$400**

Let's assume that the price of Microsoft (MSFT) is still trading around $40/share in the February expiration. If this happened the February 40 put options and the February 30 put option expire worthless, while the

116

February 50 put option has an intrinsic value of $1,000. The net profit on this trade would be $600 after you take out the net debit of $400. This is your max possible profit for this trade.

*Now let's assume that the price of Microsoft (MSFT) is trading **below $30** or **above $50** in the February expiration. If this was the case the max possible loss is limited to the initial debit on the trade. It would be limited to the initial $400 that was used to enter the trade. For this trade you are essentially risking $400 dollars to make $600. This is a good payoff.*

The long put butterfly is great to use for a stock that doesn't see too much volatility and stays within a certain range of price. If the trade happens to go against you and goes through your set price ranges it is okay because with this strategy you have fixed risk. You know how much you stand to lose prior to even getting in the trade, so there aren't any surprises when the trade happens to move against you. You have upside and downside protection.

Below is what a payoff diagram would like for a long put butterfly

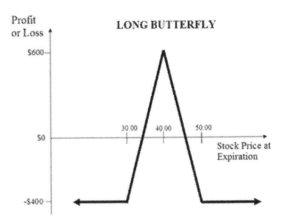

CONCLUSION

The long put butterfly is a great strategy to use if you don't think that the price of the stock will move by much and will continue to stay within a specific price range. Your focus should be on finding stocks with low volatility that aren't sensitive to major news or earnings releases.

Max Profit Potential= When the price of the stock remains unchanged

Max Loss Potential= Limited to the net debit on the trade

The iron condor is perhaps one of the most infamous options trading strategies around. It is used by many veteran traders and it is often considered one of the best strategies to minimize risk and maximize profit.

The iron condor can be a bit complex to most newbie traders and should only be used when you have a serious understanding of options and an ability to conceptualize basic strategies. Iron condors are used by many professional traders and managers. Let's see what an iron condor is and why they are so popular.

What is an Iron Condor?

An iron condor is an options trading strategy which involves four different options contracts. This strategy is meant to be used when a certain security has very low volatility or is in a period where price is consolidating. You can find these types of stock by analyzing past price trends and reading the options chain. You want to look for low implied volatility on the options chain to determine the overall volatility of a stock.

The iron condor is a limited profit and limited risk strategy. It uses a combination of put spreads and call spreads with the same expiration month with different strike prices for each.

When an iron condor is set up it will typically result in a net credit for the trade. You can have a long iron condor and a short iron condor. A long iron condor will result in a net debit, while a short iron condor will result in a net credit.

Below is how the iron condor is typically constructed.

<u>Iron Condor</u>

A long iron condor is established by selling both sides of the instrument with calls and puts and at the same time buying positions with further OTM calls and puts. The name of the position is called an iron condor because the graph resembles a large bird, like a condor.

IRON CONDOR

*= Selling 1 OTM Put Option + Buying 1 OTM Put Option **(with a lower strike price) +***
*Selling 1 OTM Call Option + Buying 1 OTM Call Option **(with a higher strike price)***

- *Sell 1 OTM Put Option*
- *Buy 1 OTM Put Option (lower strike price)*
- *Sell 1 OTM Call Option*
- *Buy 1 OTM Call Option (higher strike price)*

Benefits

Iron condors have benefits over other spread strategies because the initial margin and the maintenance margin are usually the same as other spread strategies, but the iron condor offers the benefit of **TWO NET CREDIT PREMIUMS** instead of one when compared to a traditional spread like a vertical spread (a put spread or a call spread).

This puts you at a bigger advantage to capture more profits by using a moderate amount of margin. The great thing is you don't have to babysit the trade. Iron condors have limited risk and limited profit potential and you know these before and after getting into the trade.

Scenario 1

Let's assume that McDonald's (MCD) is trading at $45/share in March. You believe that the price of McDonald's won't move very much in the next month. You decide to get into an iron condor. You execute the following 4 trades to set it up.

- Buying a **April 35 put option** for $50 (lower strike price)
- Selling a **April 40 put option** for $100 (premium received)

- Buying a **April 55 call option** for $50 (higher strike price)
- Selling a **April 50 call option** for $100 (premium received)

The net credit taken in from setting up the iron condor is $100. Let's assume that when April comes around McDonald's (MCD) is still trading around $45/share. If this were the case the 4 options contracts above would expire worthless and you get to keep your entire net credit. The net credit is your max possible profit in this scenario. You end up making $100.

Scenario 2

Let's assume that McDonald's (MCD) traded at $35/share in the April expiration instead. What would that look like? In this scenario all the options contracts would expire worthless, except the April 40 put option.

The April 40 put option has an intrinsic value of $500. In order to exit the trade, this option has to be bought back. The max possible loss here is limited to $400. This is taking the $100 credit received from entering the trade into account. This max loss is fixed even if the price of the stock goes beyond that price.

This scenario isn't the greatest payoff. You are essentially risking $400 to make $100. This type of trade will typically have a very low chance of going against you. If set up correctly, iron condors will go on to have a winning percentage of 80%-90%, depending on where you set your price ranges and targets.

The best way to set up an iron condor is to look for scenarios in the market where your max possible payoff is greater than your max possible loss. This is where the consistent profits will come from. This will take a lot of digging through options chains to find, but once you do your chances of making a profitable trade are greatly increased.

Let's take a look at what a payoff chart looks like for an iron condor for Scenario 1.

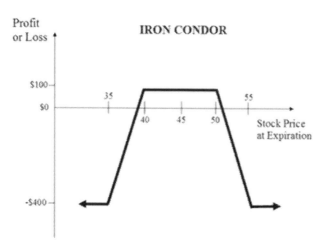

Max Profit Potential= *Limited to the Premium Taking in*

Max Loss Potential= *Limited, but can be lower or higher than the credit taken in*

Short Iron Condor

The short iron condor is essentially the opposite of a long iron condor. It is a neutral stock price strategy and is meant to be used if you believe that the price of a stock will stay around the same price.

This strategy is most similar to a **short butterfly**. A short iron condor is established by getting into a both a **bull call spread** and a **bear call spread**. Usually the premium earned for getting into this type of trade is larger than what you paid to get into it. This is the reason why short iron condors are typically a net credit transaction. The short iron condor is a limited profit and limited risk trading strategy. Let's take a look at the breakdown.

SHORT IRON CONDOR

*= Buying 1 ITM Call Option + Selling 1 ITM Call Option **(Lower Strike Price)** +*
*Buying 1 OTM Call Option + Selling 1 OTM Call Option **(Higher Strike Price)***

- *Buy 1 ITM Call Option*
- *Sell 1 ITM Call Option (lower strike price)*
- *Buy 1 OTM Call Option*
- *Sell 1 OTM Call Option (higher strike price)*

The max possible loss is incurred when the price of the stock falls between the 2 middle strike prices at expiration. Another way to think about the max possible loss is by the difference in the strike prices of the 2 lower strike calls minus the net credit that is received from the trade.

Let's take a look at the following scenarios to help us understand how the short iron condor works.

Scenario 1

Let's assume that McDonald's (MCD) is trading at $45/share in March. You believe that the price of the stock will stay around the same price and decide to get into a short iron condor. You execute the following 4 trades to set it up.

- Selling a **April 35 call option** for +$1,100
- Buying a **April 40 call option** for -$700
- Buying a **April 50 call option** for -$200
- Selling a **April 55 call option** for +$100

The net credit that is received from this trade is $300. This will be the max possible profit on this trade. Let's see what happens when the price of the stock moves to $35/share in the April expiration.

When the price of the stock goes to $35/share in the April expiration all of the options will expire worthless.

What would happen if the price of the stock went up to $55/share in the April expiration?

If this happened the **April short 55 call option** will expire worthless while the **April 40 call option** has a profit of $1,500 and the long **April 50 call option** is worth $500. This will offset the **short April 35 call option** which is worth $2,000. In this scenario you would still earn your $300 from the net credit taken in.

See the illustration below to help you understand this better if the stock price hits $55/share in the April expiration.

Net Credit taken in = **$300**   Price at expiration = $45/share

- Selling a **April 35 call option** for $1,100 = **$-2,000** at expiration
- Buying a **April 40 call option** for $700 = **$+1,500** at expiration
- Buying a **April 50 call option** for $200 = **$+500** at expiration
- Selling a **April 55 call option** for $100 = expires worthless

Net Profit = $300

($-2,000 + $1,500 + $500 +$300) = $300

Scenario 2

Let's assume that McDonald's (MCD) still traded at $45/share in the April expiration instead. What would that look like? The **April 35 call option** and **the April 40 call option** would expire in the money. The **April 40 call option** would now be worth $500 while **the April 35 call option** would be worth $1,000. Your net loss would come out to $200 in the scenario after taking the net credit into consideration. See the following breakdown to understand this further.

Net Credit taken in $300   Price at expiration = $45/share

- Selling a **April 35 call option** for $1,100 = -$,1000 at expiration
- Buying a **April 40 call option** for $700 = +$500 at expiration
- Buying a **April 50 call option** for $200 = expires worthless
- Selling a **April 55 call option** for $100 = expires worthless

Net Loss = $200

($-1,000 + $500 + **$300**) = -$200

The max possible loss for the short iron condor occurs when the price of the stock falls between the 2 middle strike prices at expiration.

Let's take a look at what a payoff chart looks like for a short iron condor for

Scenario 2.

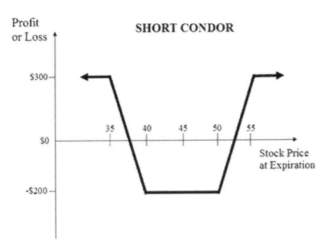

Max Profit Potential= Limited to the premium taken in

Max Loss Potential*= Limited, but can be lower or higher than the credit taken in*

In conclusion iron condors are meant to be used to profit from a stock price moving up or down which has low volatility. If you believe that the price of a stock will not move much by expiration and want fixed risk, an iron condor is the way to go. The max possible profit is limited to the net credit taken in for the trade and the max loss is limited to the net debit taken into a trade.

The benefit of an iron condor is that it can help you generate large premiums while having defined risk. It takes the guesswork out of how much you will make or lose. It also limits the margin requirements to support this type of position because the margin is limited to only one spread. Depending on how the iron condor is set up you can increase the likelihood of a profitable trade by adjusting your trades.

IRON BUTTERFLY

The iron butterfly, or commonly referred to as an iron butterfly spread or iron-fly, is another advanced options trading strategy that can be extremely profitable if done correctly. Like the iron condor, the iron butterfly is a limited risk, limited profit trading strategy that is used when an investor believes that the price of the stock will remain within a certain price range through the expiration date of the option.

The iron butterfly is different from a regular butterfly spread in two aspects; it is net credit spread upon the entry of the trade, whereas the regular butterfly spread is net debit spread upon the entry of the trade, and it requires the use of four different contracts instead of the three that are required in a regular butterfly spread.

An iron butterfly is done by combining a bear call spread along with a bull put spread with the same expiration date. The iron butterfly will have 2 wings and 2 heads.

Below is how the iron butterfly is typically constructed.

Iron Butterfly

IRON BUTTERFLY = Sell 1 ATM Put Option + Sell 1 ATM Call Option + Buy 1 OTM Put Option + Buy 1 OTM Call Option

- *Buy 1 OTM Put Option   (wing 1)*
- *Sell 1 ATM Put Option   (head of the option)*
- *Sell 1 ATM Call Option (head of the option)*
- *Buy 1 OTM Call Option   (wing 2)*

The goal with the iron butterfly is to collect some or all of the credit that is received upon entry of the trade. This will happen when the price of the stock closes between the upper and lower strike prices of the option. You want the price of the option to expire between the two wings.

The closer the price of the stock closes to the middle strike price of the option, the higher your profit. You will have a loss if the price of the stock closes either above the strike price of the upper call option or below the strike price of the lower put option.

Example

Let's assume that McDonald's (MCD) is currently trading at $40/share in January. You don't believe that that the stock will move out of a specific price range and you decide to execute an iron butterfly. You end up picking your specific price ranges and are comfortable with the amount of possible risk there is on the trade. You execute the following 4 trades to set it up.

- ***Buying 1 February 30 put option for -$50***
- *Selling 1 February 40 put option for +$300*
- *Selling 1 February 40 call option for + $300*
- ***Buying 1 February 50 call option for -$50***

For this trade you receive a net credit of $500. This is your max possible profit on this trade.

Let's assume that in the February expiration McDonald's (MCD) is still trading at around $40/share. If this was the case all 4 of the options contracts would expire worthless and you get to keep the $500 credit premium as your profit on the trade.

*On the flipside, let's assume that McDonald's (MCD) is trading at $30/share in the February expiration. If this was the case, all the options except the **February 40 put** option would expire worthless. The February 40 put option will have an intrinsic value of $1,000. The put option has to be bought back in order to get out of the trade.*

Deducting the $500 credit that was received from getting into the trade, you stand to lose a maximum of $500 on the trade. The loss would be the same amount if the stock went to $50/share in the February expiration. What would happen if the price of the stock went significantly beyond your limits? Would you lose more money? The great thing about the iron butterfly is that even if the stock price went way beyond your upper or lower strike prices, you would still lose the same amount.

Let's assume that the price of McDonald's (MCD) had fallen to $25/share in the February expiration instead of $35/share. If this was the case, only the **February 30 put option** and **the February 40 put option** would expire ITM. The **February 30 put option** has an intrinsic value of $500, while the **February 40 put option** is worth $1,500. Selling the long put option for $500, and taking the $500 credit received for entering the trade into account, you would still need to put up an additional $500 to buy back the short put option worth $1,500. In this situation your max loss would still be $500.

Let's take a look at what a payoff chart looks like for an iron butterfly

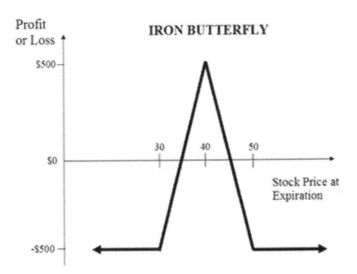

CONCLUSION

Iron butterflies can provide tremendous advantageous for options traders. Iron butterflies can be executed with a relatively small amount of margin and provide stable credit income with lower risk than one-directional spreads. The risk reward ratio is carefully defined prior to entering the trade, so you know your max loss before you even get into the trade.

The initial credit received upon entering the trade is your max possible profit on the trade. The max loss that you can incur from this strategy is when the price of the stock falls at or below the lower strike price of the put option purchased or if the price of the stock rises above or equal to the higher strike price of the call option. Another way to think about the max loss in any situation for the iron butterfly is the difference in strike price between the call options or put options minus the net credit that was received from getting into the trade.

Max Profit Potential= _Limited to the premium taken in_

Max Loss Potential= _Limited_

CHAPTER 7: GETTING STARTED

Now that you have educated yourself on options, the next step is to take action. You need to carefully evaluate your current financial situation and decide the amount of money you feel comfortable starting off with. The great thing is, you don't have to start off with a huge amount of money in order to trade options. That is one of the great benefits they offer to traders and investors.

Everyone reading this book will have different financial objectives and sensitivity to their money. I would suggest trading with an amount of money that won't impact your day to day lifestyle. Start off with a small amount of money and slowly put more in as your get more comfortable with options.

Before you begin trading options you need to ask yourself some important questions.

- How long do I plan to structure my trades for? Weekly, Multi-weekly, Monthly, or Longer
- How many options contracts do I plan on trading at once?
- What is my price range for the stocks I plan to trade? Identify your limits
- Will my trades have fixed risk or unlimited risk? I highly suggest having fixed risk for all your options trades.
- What are the commissions I am comfortable paying in order to trade options?

These are questions you need to ask yourself prior to putting a trade on. You need to have defined objectives with trading or you will fail. It is extremely imperative to identify your time horizon, price range, and risk tolerance with options. The key for long term profitability with options and building wealth is to have a plan that you follow habitually.

Let's take a look at some of the best online brokers for trading options

There are so many brokers out there that you can trade options with. I will only recommend 3. Each broker will be different in terms of fees and what sort of technology they offer.

My number one choice and the broker that I use for trading options is ......

- **INTERACTIVE BROKERS**

In terms of commissions and fees, Interactive Brokers is the best. No other broker out there can come even close to competing with them in terms of pricing. They have the lowest trading fees out of anyone out there. I absolutely love using them. They are more for the veteran day trader.

Their fees are 91% lower than the industry average. They charge $.70 per options contract and $1.0 per trade. You will struggle to find that anywhere else

I am in no way shape or form affiliated with them and am not trying to push you there. There are no affiliate links here so my opinion is simply coming from my experiencing with them. A few things to note about Interactive Brokers.

They don't offer the best customer service if you have issues setting up your account or if you have technical issues with your platform, but their trading fees more than make up for it. Their trading platform can be a little bit difficult to navigate if you are a newbie. It is built more for the experienced trader. It does however offer some very unique trading tools that most other platforms don't offer. Their minimum deposit is $10,000.

Broker number 2 that I recommend is.....

- **TRADESTATION**

Their fees are fairly competitive to Interactive Brokers. They offer excellent customer service and support. Their trading platform is very newbie friendly and the account setup process is very easy.

I have noticed that their platform is sometimes delayed in pricing and order execution can have some issues during times of high volatility. This doesn't happen very frequently, but it does happen. Despite this, they are still a very reputable broker to use. They charge $4.99 per trade and $.70 per contract. You can get your fees lowered if you trade a higher volume of contracts.

They have been around for quite some time. Their minimum deposit amount is only $500. Very attractive for newbies and people who don't want to start off with a huge amount of money.

Broker number 3 that I recommend is.....

- **TD Ameritrade**

TD Ameritrade is one of the most reputable brokers around. They have been around for longer than I have been alive. Their platform, ThinkorSwim, is one of the best platforms to use if you are complete newbie or even a veteran day trader.

Their fees are on the higher end of most brokers, but they are very reliable in terms of pricing and execution. They charge $9.99 per trade and $.75 per contract. They have top tier customer service and support. Their minimum deposit is only $500.

Everyone will start off with something different. When you begin trading, you will become very cost conscious and see how much your fees can eat into your profits. If you can't start off with Interactive Brokers, don't worry. You can slowly build your way towards that level. At the end of the day you want to minimize your trading costs as much as you possibly can.

There is a jungle out there full of resources that you can use to help you research options trades. You don't need to confuse yourself and use too many. I would recommend sticking with only three research resources. You need one for filtering, news and commentary and market research.

For filtering my stock options I use a site called www.finviz.com

They are free resource that you can use to filter the stocks you plan to trade options on. They have some awesome tools you can use for free to help you find the options that have a great market and that will be in play. I highly recommend using them.

For news and commentary I use a site called www.tastytrade.com

The guys over at Tasty Trade have built an absolutely awesome community of options traders and experts to help you learn options and stay up to date on the current market. I highly suggest sitting down a couple times a week and listening to their show. High valuable information.

For market research I use a site called www.barchart.com

Once I filter my stocks, I will either go to my trading platform or barchart.com to confirm the stocks have a good options market. Barchart.com is an amazing free service that you can use to do your research on options.

CONCLUSION

This is not the end. This is the beginning of your trading journey. There is a reason you picked up this book. Now that you have come this far, you need to take action and apply what you have learned. Trading has made many people millionaires over and over again. I am 100% confident that if you take the time to apply yourself and the lessons in this book, you can achieve financial freedom. It won't be easy, but it is more than possible. Your success is up to you.

Will you stay up late and find those hidden trades that will shower you with easy profits? Will you do the research that no one else is doing? Will you master strategies that are complicated, but extremely profitable? Will you dedicate yourself to options so you can live a prosperous life?

Only you know the answers.

Become obsessed with knowledge and knowledge will yield you freedom.

21019248R00082

Printed in Poland
by Amazon Fulfillment
Poland Sp. z o.o., Wrocław